THE SMALL RURAL PARISH

The Small Rural Parish

BERNARD QUINN

THE PARISH PROJECT / NCCB   GLENMARY RESEARCH CENTER
New York   Washington, D.C.

GRC A-64/P-3
January, 1980

THE PARISH PROJECT grew out of a concern of the American bishops for the quality of parish life in the United States. It is an endeavor that hopes to discover qualities of effective parishes and ways of helping parish ministry by critically reflecting and acting upon the pastoral experience of clergy, religious and laity.

THE GLENMARY RESEARCH CENTER was established in 1966 to help serve the research needs of the Catholic Church in rural America.

IMPRIMATUR: Msgr. John F. Donoghue, Vicar General, Archdiocese of Washington, September 27, 1979. *Nihil obstat*: Msgr. Antioquino Arroyo, Censor Deputatus.

AVAILABLE from The Parish Project, National Conference of Catholic Bishops, 299 Elizabeth St., New York, N.Y. 10012, and the Glenmary Research Center, 4606 East-West Highway, Washington, D.C. 20014.

To Pastors,

without whose wisdom and dedication the vision described in these pages cannot be transformed into reality

Contents

Foreword

A characteristic of any approach to parish development must be awareness of the differences among parishes. These differences arise from the history of the people, the history of church life in the area, the demographic characteristics of the parish, and the locale. Thus there are sharp differences between urban parishes in traditionally Catholic areas and rural parishes where Catholics constitute a relatively small portion of the total population. And, it might be added, parishes in rural areas where the population is largely Catholic differ from those where the population is largely Protestant. Another major distinction among parishes is their size: the total number of people, the size of the staff, and the geographic area included.

In this book Father Quinn looks specifically at the small rural parish and draws on experience largely in areas where Catholics are a minority. This focus and his experience makes the book very practically helpful. At the same time, he situates the practical ingredients clearly in a theological viewpoint. This viewpoint includes as part of parish life the development of people, the ecumenical aspects of ministry, and the necessary foundation of parish ministry in increasingly conscious faith. The book also emphasizes the relationship between parish *community* and the *mission* of the Church. The community is assembled and gathered; it also reaches out to others.

The Parish Project of the National Conference of Catholic Bishops is delighted to be associated with this contribution to one major form of parish life: the small rural parish.

REV. PHILIP J. MURNION
Director, The Parish Project
National Conference of Catholic Bishops

Preface

Several years ago, in an essay entitled *Toward a Job Description for the Nonmetropolitan Parish*, I suggested that the work of the parish might benefit from the development of "middle-range principles" that could bridge the gap between the general vision of ministry that theology provides, and the actual practice of that ministry. I tentatively sketched a few examples of such principles and pointed out how they could be used to gain perspective on even the most humble parochial activities. The response to the idea encouraged me to pursue it further, stimulating an intellectual journey that has led to the writing of this book.

Because I am working in what I call the middle range, the reader will find neither an abstract treatise on the parish nor a "how-to" pastoral manual. I hope, though, that my very real enthusiasm for parochial ministry will show through on these pages. Naturally, most of that enthusiasm stems from what the parish *is*. But part of it flows from what the parish *is not*. There is a whole range of tasks which cannot reasonably be assigned to the local

Eucharistic community in today's world. Once released from these tasks it is free to become what the Church truly wants it to be.

The principles I suggest are developed in the context of the small rural parish. Other people will have to judge the extent to which they apply to large parishes or urban situations; my own research and experience have been limited entirely to rural America. Further, my concern is with the "what" rather than the "who" of parish ministry. While I affirm the critical role of the pastor and the need for active participation by religious and laity, the relationships among all these ministers are not explored. I have chosen to focus on the *ministry* in which they are collectively engaged.

I wish to thank my colleague, David Byers, for editing this manuscript and for offering advice and assistance in a number of ways. I am also especially grateful to all those thoughtful rural leaders—priests, religious and laypeople—whose insights and gentle criticisms have challenged and disciplined my thought.

I
Introduction

JUST AS A LIVING ORGANISM undergoes constant change, a Catholic parish passes through stages of development marked by progress or regression, success or failure, growth or decline. This book is about the early life and growth of a rural parish—one that is still small and not yet a vital, self-sustaining Eucharistic community firmly rooted in its locality.

During its formative years a parish is necessarily a part of the Church's "missionary activity," because, with a helping hand from the outside, it is struggling to become a viable Catholic presence among the people in a given place. During this missionary period, three formative stages in the life of a rural parish can be discerned; these are quite distinct from the later stages of parish development which lie beyond the scope of this book. In the first stage, which I have called "initial gathering," people are called together to form a congregation. As the parish grows in size and spirituality, it enters the second or "intensification" stage and begins organized ministries to the community at large. In the third stage, "localiza-

1

tion," it penetrates all major social groupings and becomes truly indigenous to the local area.

Since its spiritual and material resources obviously become more extensive as it progresses from stage to stage, the parish's expectations and priorities should be different· even though, theologically speaking, its basic task remains the same. In accomplishing that task a parish faces many problems and challenges, both in its internal life as a congregation and in its outreach to the community at large. The way it meets these challenges in its formative stages, the direction it consciously or unconsciously chooses, will to a great extent determine what it becomes in the future—in twenty, fifty or a hundred years.

I begin this discussion of the small rural congregation by commenting on the general nature of the parish, describing the characteristics of the 862 mission counties of the United States served by small parishes or none at all, and pointing out how rural ministry differs in context from ministry in urban areas. Chapter II describes seven of the challenges the developing parish faces—those which I believe to be the most critical, based on my experience as a rural pastor and more than a decade of field study at the Glenmary Research Center. Some challenges relate to the nurture of the congregation: its community life, its focus on Christ, and its sense of Catholic identity. Others involve the parish's outreach to the community at large: ecumenism, evangelization, social action and concern for the wider Church. Finally, Chapter III examines the three formative stages of parish development in broad perspective, outlining the priorities and expectations appropriate to each.

My purpose, then, is to set forth the elements of a dynamic. What is a parish? Against the backdrop of rural America, what should a parish strive to become? How does it get from the point of initial establishment to a level of development that makes it a true indigenous presence of the Church? I will be content if this book makes some contribution to the search for answers to these questions.

THE PARISH

Americans live in a society increasingly dominated by large-scale organizations, each dealing with a narrow segment of human life. We shop in department stores, we buy cars from General Motors, we vote in national elections. Most of us, however, practice our religion through small-scale communities that are not at all specialized—"parishes" in current Catholic usage.[1] One of the distinguishing characteristics of a parish is that it serves the broad range of people's elementary and basic religious needs. Its concern is with everyday life as a whole, rather than with any particular, specialized dimension. It is the place of the baptismal font, the regular commemoration of the Lord's death and resurrection, the preaching of the word, the formation of consciences, the nurture of Christian callings, the celebration of the major events of life, the inspiration for witness to the world outside.

1. In this book the word "parish" also includes what the *Official Catholic Directory* calls a "mission," that is, a congregation which constitutes a subgrouping within a canonically established parish. Missions usually have church buildings; they do not often have a resident priest.

The Church does manifest its presence in specialized ways, of course: Catholic colleges provide advanced education, hospitals and clinics serve the sick, large-scale ministries of justice address urgent social needs, neighborhood centers serve the poor, contemplative houses offer constant praise to God.[2] But the parish is unique precisely in its *generality*. It offers the comprehensive setting needed for ordinary, everyday Christian witness and life.[3]

As an official local community within the universal Church, the parish contains all the basic elements that Catholic life requires—the Sacraments, teaching authority, the pastoral office, and the baptismal ministries of comfort, challenge, evangelization, witness and service. Among these endowments, the Eucharist has always assumed the greatest importance. "No Christian community . . . is built up unless it has its basis and center in the celebration of the Most Holy Eucharist. . . ."[4] So central is the Eucharist to Catholic life that the parish is

2. In Appendix B, I suggest a classification of non-parochial (correlative) ministries. For a discussion about the relationship between parochial and non-parochial ministries, see Karl Rahner, "Peaceful Reflections on the Parochial Principle," *Theological Investigations*, vol. II (Baltimore: Helicon, 1963), pp. 283 ff. See also David Byers, *New Directions for the Rural Church: Case Studies in Area Ministry* (New York: Paulist Press, 1978).

3. Yves Congar suggests a correlary: "Whatever requires the employment of large and varied resources and extensive cooperation, or concerns a particular way of Christian life, should be taken out of the parochial framework." *A Gospel Priesthood* (New York: Herder and Herder, 1967), p. 159.

4. Vatican II, *Decree on the Ministry and Life of Priests*, n. 6. The same decree also states (n. 5): "The other Sacraments, as well as every ministry of the Church and every work of the apostolate, are linked with the holy Eucharist and are directed toward it. For the most blessed Eucharist contains the Church's entire spiritual wealth, that is, Christ Himself, our Passover and living bread. Through His very flesh, made vital and vitalizing by the Holy Spirit; He offers life to men. They are thereby invited and led to offer themselves, their labors, and all created things together with Him."

often called a "Eucharistic community."[5]

In our time, the territorial parish is the most common form. People belong to St. John's or St. Mary's because they live within the boundaries the diocese has established. While I think the rationale for the territorial parish is especially sound,[6] I would not like to give the impression that it is the only workable model. There are parishes whose membership is determined by nationality, by migrant or student status, by institutional residence, by occupation, or even, in certain circumstances, by personal choice.[7] None is excluded from the present discussion.

Whatever its organizational form, however, the parish is inclusive rather than restrictive in membership: it is composed of baptized Catholics[8] of all levels of commit-

5. For example, see Casiano Floristan, *La paroisse: communauté eucharistique* (Paris: P. Lethielleux, 1963), p. 153.

6. My opinion is based on the advantages of a system whereby some organization in the Church, at least theoretically, has responsibility for ministry to everyone. Screwtape provides an additional perspective: "... the parochial organization should always be attacked, because, being a unity of place and not of likings, it brings people of different classes and psychology together in the kind of unity the Enemy desires." C. S. Lewis, *The Screwtape Letters* (London: Geoffrey Bles, 1942), p. 81.

7. Alex Blöchlinger says: "There is no theology of [the present] concrete form of the parish as such, except for the wholly general statement that the Church must become localized and to a large extent adopt human social structures. For the concrete form of the parish as such has no specific or essential relationship with the supernatural reality of the Church apart from the necessary localization and incarnational structure, neither of which necessitates just this particular form of parish." *The Modern Parish Community* (New York: P. J. Kenedy, 1965), p. 147. See also Salvador Pons Franco, *Parroquia y misión en la eclesiología del Vatican II* (Alcoy: Marfil, 1970), pp. 213-236. The concrete form of the parish, in its various manifestations, is determined by canon law. See Canons 216, 451 ff., and 1350.

8. Baptism is the most general foundation for membership in the parish, since it constitutes the basis for incorporation into the Church. Vatican II states: "Incorporated into the Church through baptism, the faithful are destined by the baptismal character for the worship of the Christian religion; reborn as sons of God they must confess before men the faith which they have received from God through the Church." *Dogmatic Constitution on the Church*, n. 11.

ment. It is not a "covenant" community like a religious order, whose membership is restricted to those willing to accept a particular way of Christian life. In the Catholic (as opposed to the Free Church) system, the local congregation is open even to those with minimal faith and practice.

The ideal parish is not just a service center where people come as individuals to receive the ministrations of the priest. More and more, the parish is being viewed not merely as a collection of individuals, but as a community of love and service.[9] True community implies mutual relationships, a division of labor, and a sense of interdependence in working toward common goals. In an ecclesial community the pastor's role, although crucial, cannot be the only active one. All members of the congregation— priests, religious, lay—are called to minister to one another according to the charisms, offices, graces and spiritual powers that each has received.[10]

While the parish is concerned with the needs of its own members, it has strong ties to the outside world as well. It reaches out to other Christians as individuals and to non-Catholic ecclesial communions, seeking "the unity which the Lord desires." It cares for the spiritual welfare of the unchurched, those whose values are not rein-

---

9. As Blöchlinger points out, the present canon law makes no express statement about the parish as a community, although it contains all the elements necessary for one. *The Modern Parish Community*, p. 119. The 1977 draft of the new *Code of Canon Law* is more explicit: "A parish is a determined portion of the people of God constituted in a particular Church...." Canon 349. In addition, Vatican II clearly refers to the parish as a community. See, for example, *Decree on the Ministry and Life of Priests* (n. 6): "The office of pastor is not confined to the care of the faithful as individuals, but is also properly extended to the formation of a genuine Christian community."

10. See Vatican II, *Decree on the Apostolate of the Laity*, n. 10

forced through participation in any local religious group. It extends itself in ministries of mercy and justice, especially on behalf of the poor. And it broadens its apostolate beyond the local horizon through involvement in the mission of the diocese, the nation and the universal Church.[11]

In doing all this the parish offers a ministry of both comfort and challenge. It proclaims a gospel that lifts up, ennobles and helps with burdens. But it also proclaims a gospel that disturbs—intruding on human consciousness and culture, calling for individual and collective response. Thus the parish, in its corporate life as well as in the lives of its members, participates in the mystery of the cross. At times it is called upon to sacrifice some measure of institutional well-being for the sake of the gospel message. Trusting in the unseen power of God, however, it confidently expects the triumph of the resurrection both now and in the time to come.

The parish contains not only visible elements, but invisible ones as well. The Lord has promised, "Where two or three are gathered together for my sake, there am I in the midst of them" (Mt 18:20). Like any Christian group, the parish can count on God's grace to enlighten the common decisions, strengthen the common actions, and uphold the common goals. To say this is not to deny the possibility of group unfaithfulness, even group sin. The conscience of a community is no more immune from error than the conscience of an individual. The reverse

11. Canon 1350, for example, assigns responsibility to the parish for all non-Catholics residing within the parish boundaries. See also Vatican II: *Decree on the Bishops' Pastoral Office in the Church*, n. 30; *Decree on the Apostolate of the Laity*, n. 10; *Decree on Priestly Formation*, n. 2.

is also true, however. God is present not only in the actions of individuals, but also in their common undertakings as members of a group.

This, then, is what I mean by parish: *a local Eucharistic community of baptized Catholics with various levels of commitment, whose members, with the Lord's help, serve one another's ordinary, everyday religious needs and reach out in witness to the community at large.* It is a basic building block of the universal Church, designed, above all, to make religion an integral part of people's lives.

In recent years the parish has been attacked repeatedly on the grounds that it no longer fulfills its essential mission. Some would say, "The parish is dead. Let us stop waving the hand of a corpse at the people who pass by."[12] Human weakness and lack of vision affect the parish, as they do every institution. But that need not dampen our enthusiasm for a ministry that furthers God's work, however slowly and haltingly, in the context of the ordinary and the everyday. Other apostolates are important and even essential for the Church's life.[13] It is my firm conviction, however, that the Church's vitality depends in the long run on the vitality of the local parish.

---

12. Martin E. Marty discusses criticisms of the parish in *Death and Birth of the Parish* (St. Louis: Concordia, 1964), pp. 3-26.

13. On this point, Pope Paul VI stated: "All of you are well aware that Vatican II retained and confirmed the nobility of the parochial structure, as the normal and primary expression of pastoral care. In itself, however, it is not sufficient to meet all the modern needs. Many other forms of apostolate are necessary in order to bring the word and grace of the gospel into the center of man's life today; there are many other forms of religious witness, in the cultural, educational, and recreational spheres, which cannot have the parish as their point of departure...." *L'Osservatore Romano,* September 10, 1966. See also Appendix B.

MISSION AREAS

Jesus commanded His disciples to carry His message "to the very ends of the earth" (Mt 28:18). Simply carrying the message, however, is not enough. If the gospel is to have a lasting impact on people's lives, it must be embodied in some concrete structure. For this reason, gathering and developing local Eucharistic communities has traditionally been a central element in the Church's missionary task.[14]

In some ways the Church is present in a given area even before a parish exists. It may be present through the witness of Catholic families who reside there; through media coverage of a papal statement or a church-sponsored housing program; through the work of regional hospitals or colleges; or through local organized apostolates of prayer, justice, social service and the like. Until a local Eucharistic community springs up, however, the Church is not fully present. The people do not yet have practical access to all the elements of ordinary Catholic life.

As a whole, the United States is hardly a mission country. The Church has taken firm root here and has established itself in every part of the land. Most people simply accept this fact as a given, and are surprised to learn that there are 288 American counties completely without parishes or missions where Sunday Mass is regularly celebrated. If the 2,888,237 residents of those counties want to worship God in a Catholic community, they must cross

---

14. "The Church ... continues unceasingly to send heralds of the gospel until such time as the infant churches are fully established and can themselves continue the work of evangelizing." Vatican II, *Dogmatic Constitution on the Church*, n. 17.

county lines to do so, often traveling many miles (Figure 1).

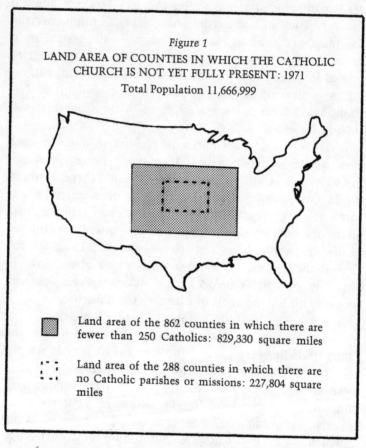

Figure 1
LAND AREA OF COUNTIES IN WHICH THE CATHOLIC
CHURCH IS NOT YET FULLY PRESENT: 1971
Total Population 11,666,999

Land area of the 862 counties in which there are fewer than 250 Catholics: 829,330 square miles

Land area of the 288 counties in which there are no Catholic parishes or missions: 227,804 square miles

While 288 counties are unserved, 574 others are underserved. Here parishes or missions do exist, but the number of Catholics is so small (less than 250) that it is difficult for the congregation to maintain a full program of ministries.[15] Sometimes Christian education for each age group is an impossibility; sometimes the Sunday liturgy is undeveloped; often there is no parish council. Since the Catholics living in these counties make up only 0.6 percent of the total local population, the congregation's potential impact in ecumenism, evangelization and social outreach is not great enough to constitute a full and effective Catholic presence.

In all, 862 counties containing 11,666,999 people either have no Catholic community or one that is only in an embryonic stage of development.[16] These are the "mission counties," and 80 percent of them are in Appalachia, the South, and the South Central regions of the United States (Figure 2). Moreover, the 33 mission counties of the Southwest are clustered along its eastern rim, an area that has much in common with the states of the neighboring South Central region. When I speak of mission territory, then, I am referring primarily to a slice of America extending south from Virginia and West Virginia, and run-

15. Hervé Carrier says: "An overly reduced population hampers the cohesion and the stability of religious participation. . . . The parish is a ritual community and because of this it requires stable institutions, a pastoral organization, and permanent social structures which will assure the functioning of parish service. The permanence of the institution, or at least its orderly functioning, would be compromised by the extremely small size of the parish group. . . . The extreme diversity of situations prevents the determination of any precise figures. The principle, however, will be retained: the parish, being a worshipping community, needs dimensions which render it viable as an institution." *The Sociology of Religious Belonging* (New York: Herder and Herder, 1965), p. 204. The Glenmary Missioners employ the figure of 250 parishioners to indicate a viable congregation. This figure was selected in consultation with ordinaries of ten U.S. dioceses containing extensive mission areas.

16. Religious statistics are adapted from Douglas W. Johnson, Paul R. Picard and Bernard Quinn, *Churches and Church Membership in the United States: An Enumeration by Region, State and County 1971* (Washington, D.C.: Glenmary Research Center, 1974). Population figures are from the U.S. Census 1970.

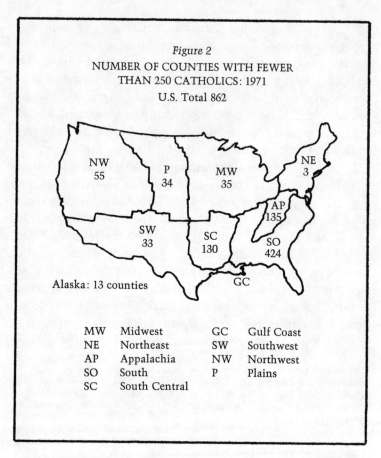

Figure 2
NUMBER OF COUNTIES WITH FEWER
THAN 250 CATHOLICS: 1971
U.S. Total 862

MW	Midwest	GC Gulf Coast
NE	Northeast	SW Southwest
AP	Appalachia	NW Northwest
SO	South	P Plains
SC	South Central	

ning west to Texas. The only other concentrated mission area is in the Northwest, where most of the 55 counties with slight Catholic presence lie in the heavily Mormon sections of Idaho and Utah. The 72 mission counties scattered through the remaining regions represent exceptional circumstances about which it is difficult to generalize.

The task of planting a Eucharistic community in a particular area must be approached with the same creative attention to local realities that is found in the best tradition of missionary activity in the Church.[17] The first of these realities is the *religious atmosphere*—one that is alien to, and somewhat unsympathetic towards, the Catholic ethos.[18] Conservative evangelicals predominate in Appalachia, the South, and the South Central regions. Catholics here must strive to preserve their identity in the face of the surrounding culture; foster dialogue with evangelicals, who have a different idea of church cooperation than their more ecumenical counterparts in other regions; minister to unchurched people whose image of religion is likely to have been formed by the evangelical experience; and address social issues in the context of evangelical reservations about church participation in secular affairs. The same conditions, with different nuances, apply in the Mormon areas of the Northwest.

The second reality is the presence of the *unchurched*. Of the 11.7 million people who live in the mission counties of America, 4.3 million are unchurched. While these people might profess some Christian beliefs, they do not partici-

17. For a detailed description of the religious and social characteristics of the regions containing the bulk of the mission counties, see Bernard Quinn and John Feister, *Apostolic Regions of the United States: 1971* (Washington, D.C.: Glenmary Research Center, 1978). The statistics given in the following paragraphs were adapted from this publication, or from the sources indicated in the previous footnote.

18. The Church offers no apology for localizing Catholic communities even in places where the majority are committed, practicing Protestants. The Church is neither defensive about her own unique witness nor competitive with other communions, whose ecclesial elements she affirms. Catholics are to work toward ending the scandal of disunity among Christians; this can hardly be done at the local level unless Eucharistic communities are present. See Vatican II: *Dogmatic Constitution on the Church*, n. 17; *Decree on Ecumenism*, nn. 2-4.

pate in any local Judaeo-Christian group. The percent of the unchurched in these counties (37.1) is no higher than in the rest of the nation; in fact, except for Appalachia, it is generally lower. Ministering to such a large number of people, however, presents an awesome challenge.

The third reality is the *socio-economic situation*. The regions in which most of the mission counties are located contain several distinct, self-conscious racial and ethnic groups. Blacks constitute 25.7 percent of the rural population in the South and 14 percent in the South Central region; Hispanic people and American Indians are numerically strong in some counties of the South Central and the Southwest. Each group's approach to religion is different; somehow the parish must find a way to meet their special needs, while continuing to serve the people in the cultural majority.

Most of the mission counties are beginning to recover from four decades of population decline; from 1970 to 1977 their overall population increased by 10.1 percent.[19] In spite of this growth (in a few cases, because of it), social problems abound. In comparison to the nation as a whole, for example, the educational level in mission counties is low, poverty is high, housing is substandard, and health services are poor.[20] In addition, there are prob-

19. County population statistics for 1977 are from the *Commercial Atlas and Marketing Guide 1977* (Chicago: Rand McNally, 1977). See also Calvin L. Beale, *The Revival of Population Growth in Nonmetropolitan America* (Washington, D.C.: Economic Research Service, U.S. Department of Agriculture, 1975).

20. In the nation as a whole, one person in 20 is illiterate, one family in ten has an income below the poverty level, and one person in 20 lives in substandard housing. In mission areas, one person in four is illiterate; one family in four has an income below the poverty level, and one person in four lives in substandard housing. U.S. Census 1970.

lems relating to land use, agricultural production, soil conservation, energy, transportation, legal services, political empowerment, industrial relations, community development, and the needs of minorities, youth, the aging, migrants, factory workers, miners and farmers. No mission parish will run out of subjects for social action.

THE RURAL CONTEXT

By far the most significant characteristic of the mission counties in the United States is their rural quality. Slightly over 93 percent of the people live in open countryside or in towns of less than 10,000, away from cities, suburbs and urban fringes.[21] The typical mission parish, then, will develop in the context of rural society. Is there anything about ministry in a rural setting that sets it apart from ministry in a suburb or city?

This question requires a complex answer. Theologically, of course, there is no difference; the tasks the Church has given the parish are the same everywhere. Further, American life is becoming increasingly homogenized. As Sherwood Anderson once said, "The invisible roofs of the towns and cities are extending out to cover the world."[22] Part of the reason is mass communications. The cosmopolitan outlook characteristic of city people is often found

21. U.S. Census 1970. In setting the upper limit of rural settlement at 10,000, I am following the opinion of Lofland, who states, "... once the population of the settlement reaches 8,000 to 10,000 persons, the transition to the city has occurred." Lofland's opinion is based on the nature of interpersonal relationships in places above and below that size. Lyn H. Lofland, *A World of Strangers: Order and Action in Urban Public Space* (New York: Basic Books, 1973), p. 11.

22. Sherwood Anderson, *Poor White* (New York: Viking Press, 1920), p. 129.

among rural people as well, since everyone is watching the same programs and hearing the same news from the same sources. The ease of modern transportation is also a powerful factor in the blurring of urban and rural differences. People in small towns travel far and wide to work, to shop, to visit, to recreate.[23] Between 1965 and 1970, one out of every six rural Americans changed their county of residence.[24] Such mobility has dispelled the isolation on which much of the past uniqueness of rural life was based.

The change in our small towns and open countryside is most evident in the dramatic shift away from local interdependence.[25] A century ago, a farmer would call on his neighbors instead of an insurance company to rebuild his burned-out barn. Old and infirm people would rely more on their relatives than on Social Security. And a hamburger would be provided by Joe's Sandwich Shop rather than by a complex international organization capable of producing 26 billion other hamburgers. The mutual dependence of neighbors, workers and business people was highly visible and a source of security. In rural America the day has long passed when this kind of relationship is possible.

23. The increase in the radius of rural contacts has been well documented. For a bibliography see Dean R. Yoesting and D. G. Marshall, "Trade Pattern Changes of Open-Country Residents: A Longitudinal Study," *Rural Sociology*, 34:1 (March, 1969), 85-91.

24. U.S. Census 1970.

25. An expanded theoretical presentation of this point will be found in Roland L. Warren, *The Community in America* (Chicago: Rand McNally, 1963). Arthur J. Vidich and Joseph Bensman describe the same phenomenon in their classic case study, *Small Town in Mass Society* (Princeton, New Jersey: Princeton University Press, 1968). See also Bernard Quinn, *The Changing Context of Town and Country Ministry* (Washington, D.C.: Glenmary Research Center, 1970).

If the small town in today's mass society is no longer the classic, traditional "community" described by Tönnies, Durkheim and others, it is still different in important ways from the city.[26] The average density of our urban population is 210 people per square mile; in rural areas it is 18 per square mile, since towns are small and scattered.[27] One consequence of this settlement pattern is that rural people are in closer daily contact with the rhythms of nature than city people are.[28] If the preaching of the gospel is to take its starting point from people's lives, the use of the images of nature in the liturgy and in homilies will assume a certain importance.

A second consequence is the distance that rural people have to travel to meet one another and participate in organized groups. In one place in Nebraska, for example, the members of a parish council are required to travel a combined total of more than 1500 miles every time they meet. The way a rural parish operates will be strongly affected by the distance factor.

The effects of low population density are most obvious, perhaps, in the way rural people tend to relate to one another. Visitors walking down Main Street in Turkeyfoot, Arkansas get a different feeling than they do when walking down Madison Avenue in New York. All the residents

26. See John C. McKinney and Charles P. Loomis, "The Typological Tradition," in Ferdinand Tönnies, *Community and Society* (New York: Harper & Row, 1957), pp. 12-29; and Robert A. Nisbet, *Community and Power* (New York: Oxford University Press, 1962).

27. U.S. Census 1970.

28. It is true that city people are spending more leisure time in rural places than ever before. But there is a difference between visiting the country and actually living there, just as there is a difference between visiting the city and becoming an urban resident.

of Turkeyfoot know one another, and a stranger is recognized as a stranger. There are some places in rural America where this is not true, of course, just as there are certain urban ethnic neighborhoods where it is. But because rural living involves relatively small clusters of people, it tends to favor the development of what might be called "communities of mutual recognition."

A distinct social dynamic is likely to develop in such communities. The people may not all be friends or intimates, but they relate to one another in a rather complex and personal way. For example, Jesse Stuart tells how his grandparents ran a general store in Three Prong Valley, Kentucky. Grandma was a Democrat and Methodist, and Grandpa a Republican and Baptist. "Grandpa refused to wait on the Democrats and Methodists and Grandma waited on them. But Grandma wouldn't wait on the Baptists and Republicans, so Grandpa waited on them and would let them have anything, whether the credit was good or not."[29]

In Three Prong Valley a business transaction was something personal. A clerk in a city supermarket, on the other hand, simply cannot relate to the hundreds of people who pass through the checkout counter as individuals. He does not even know most of them and sees them primarily as customers, touching their lives in only one role among the many that make up their total personalities. City people typically confine their personal relationships to their circle of family and friends; business contacts tend to be

29. Jesse Stuart, *My Land Has a Voice* (New York: McGraw-Hill, 1966), p. 64.

highly specialized and to lack human depth.[30] In small towns, however, there is little occasion to separate business from the ordinary flow of social life.

Rural relationships are generally not only more personal in character, but more mutual in extent: *the people who know you also know one another.* The individual immersed in such interlocking relationships is both assured of a niche in the social universe and pressured to conform to community standards. The pressure is so strong at times that Edgar Howe could define the rural community as "the place where you hear gossip about your sins on the way home from committing them."[31] To the extent that these mutual relationships are long-standing, the community may take on the semblance of a private club. Newcomers, even after years of residence, sometimes feel they have not yet been invited to join.

These human networks are crucial for effective ministry, and the rural parish ignores them at its peril. A personal quality should characterize the way the parish serves its own members and the community at large. This quality can only be realized if the leadership is sensitive to the social patterns in which parishioners move, whether or not

30. Louis Wirth has provided the classic description of urban relationships: "Characteristically, urbanites meet one another in highly segmental roles. They are, to be sure, dependent upon more people for the satisfactions of their life-needs than are rural people and thus are associated with a greater number of organized groups, but they are less dependent upon particular persons, and their dependence upon others is confined to a highly fractionalized aspect of the other's round of activity. This is essentially what is meant by saying that the city is characterized by secondary rather than primary contacts. The contacts of the city may indeed be face to face, but they are nevertheless impersonal, superficial, transitory, and segmental." Albert J. Reiss, Jr., ed., *Louis Wirth on Cities and Social Life* (Chicago: University of Chicago Press, 1974), p. 71.

31. Edgar W. Howe, *Plain People* (New York: Dodd, Mead, 1929), p. 305.

these patterns are coextensive with the official parochial structure. The mutuality of relationships also tends to encourage a certain informality of style that has carried over from simpler days. Our great grandfathers in rural America rarely sent memoranda to one another in duplicate; they leaned over the cracker barrel and indulged in knowing winks. I am not suggesting that modern rural parishes can operate with cracker barrel informality or that they can dispense with organizational tools. But important tasks can still be handled in a rather relaxed way.

The small town has often been compared to a fishbowl, and not without reason.[32] A congregation serving a small community cannot expect the anonymity or privacy characteristic of city life. Enmities within the parish, plans and goals, attitudes, everyday activities, good deeds and scandals will all become common knowledge. Because of the interlocking relationships, the channels of informal communication are well lubricated; the opportunities for positive as well as negative witness are accordingly much greater.

It follows that rural ministry requires a communal approach. The individual is not served in isolation, or as a member of various unrelated groups. It is the community as a whole whose influence on the individual is decisive, and whom the individual influences in turn. In serving one person, therefore, ministers will keep one eye on all those cousins, uncles, aunts, acquaintances and associates who are, so to speak, peering over a person's shoulder, and will take them very much into account.

32. Sinclair Lewis's *Main Street* provides an excellent description of this dimension of rural life (New York: Harcourt, Brace and World, 1920).

II
Seven Challenges

ALL SEVEN CHALLENGES facing the rural mission parish may be summed up in one: *to provide for the spiritual nurture of its own members and to reach out in witness to the community at large.* The parish must breathe in and out (Figure 3). It must not become so exclusively turned in on itself that its inner life atrophies for want of outlet. On the other hand, it must not become so caught up in outreach that, by neglecting its own nurture, it becomes sounding brass or tinkling cymbal (1 Cor 13:1).

The first three challenges relate to *nurture*: forming community, seeking a center in Christ, and strengthening Catholic identity. The rest relate to *outreach*: advancing Christian unity, evangelizing the unchurched, carrying out social ministry, and expressing catholicity (concern for the wider Church). Although in the abstract the seven challenges have application to any parish in any setting, I will confine myself to explaining their precise relevance for parishes in the rural mission areas of the United States.

21

Figure 3
NURTURE AND OUTREACH

NOURISHED on the Sacraments and the Word of God, the Catholic community REACHES OUT in ecumenism, evangelization of the unchurched, social action and concern for the universal Church

Challenge 1

COMMUNITY

To make the parish the type of community that simultaneously fosters religious growth among its members and projects a sense of welcome to people on the outside

THE PARISH AS AN INCLUSIVE COMMUNITY

The rural mission parish is made up of saints and sinners, rich and poor, men and women, young and old, clergy and laity, conservatives and liberals, newcomers and natives. Can the lion lie down with the lamb? Can all these people, with their diverse mentalities, experiences, life styles and levels of commitment, actually be gathered into a spiritual fellowship of brothers and sisters in Christ? Relying on God's power, can they create a local Eucharistic community that is based on something more than formal participation in obligatory religious practices? That will be at the same time ecumenically responsible and fully Catholic? That will reach out to welcome people of every background and social class? That will undertake ministries of justice and mercy in the community at large?

The task will not be easy, but one thing is clear: if the parish intends to involve all these diverse people in what it aims to do, the type of community[1] that it seeks for itself

1. The word "community" is defined in a wide variety of ways. For the history of the concept as employed by sociologists, see: George A. Hillery, Jr., "Definitions of Community: Areas of Agreement," *Rural Sociology*, 20:2 (June, 1955), 111-123; George A. Hillery, Jr., *Communal Organizations: A Study of*

must be appropriate for an all-inclusive group. It simply cannot hope to achieve the closeness of community that is possible with a more restricted, or "covenant" group.

In the Church there are many covenanted organizations—religious orders, lay institutes, prayer groups, "base communities"—whose members, in one way or another, pledge themselves to a definite level of commitment to the Lord and to the group.[2] But the parish is not one of them. Although it often *contains* covenanted organizations, its own membership is more inclusive. Every parish has people who lead solid spiritual lives, who breathe vitality into parish activities, who help to make the parish an effective instrument for the Lord's work. But everyone knows that not all parishioners, not even the majority of them, are like that.[3] In the parish, there has to be room for the majority; no baptized Catholic may be excluded. More than any other structure in the Church, the parish is the net containing different varieties of fish.

Some members of the congregation are unable to participate as much as they would like because of physical disability, illness, or a family responsibility that keeps

Local Societies (Chicago: University of Chicago Press, 1968); Robert A. Nisbet, "Community" in *The Sociological Tradition* (New York: Basic Books, 1966), pp. 47-106. For opinions about the extent to which the word may be applied to a parish, see Émile Pin, *La paroisse catholique* (Rome: Gregorian University, 1963), pp. 47 ff.; Evelyn Whitehead, "The Structure of Community," in Evelyn Whitehead, ed., *The Parish in Community and Ministry* (New York: Paulist Press, 1978), pp. 37 ff.

2. For comments on "base communities" and their relationship to the parish, see Karl Rahner, "Théologie et spiritualité de la pastorale," *Nouvelle Revue Théologique*, (May-June, 1979), 381-394; P. J. Kerkhofs, "Basic Communities in the Church," *Pro Mundi Vita Bulletin*, 62 (September, 1976), p. 30; Pope Paul VI, *On Evangelization in the Modern World*, n. 58.

3. Joseph Fichter categorizes parishioners as nuclear, modal, marginal, and dormant, according to their degree of church involvement. See *Social Relations in the Urban Parish* (University of Chicago Press, 1954).

them close to home. Others might be heavily involved in church-related social action programs; charismatic, Cursillo or Marriage Encounter groups; or diocesan programs that are not formally tied to the parish. The people who are active in extra-parochial apostolates are often the most active in the parish as well. Even when these apostolates absorb time and talent that the parish would otherwise be able to draw upon, however, the parish must encourage and support such participation.

There are times when people need to stand apart from all group association and reassess their personal relationship with the Lord. This is not so much a rejection of community as a longing for elbow room during a particular stage of an individual's spiritual development. The parish must respect these legitimate needs, and look forward to eventually welcoming such persons back into greater participation in group life.

At another level, there are the religious loners who are devoted to Christ and the Church, but see little value in anything beyond a minimal involvement in the local parish. Their attitude might stem from any number of things: a naturally reserved disposition, a sense of social inferiority, a conviction that religion is inherently a private affair. With patience, they can be brought to see that devotion implies giving as well as receiving. They benefit from the local Eucharistic community and have a responsibility to contribute to it.

Then there are those who for one reason or another have been alienated from the parish, even though they have no intention of giving up the practice of their religion. Perhaps they are uncomfortable with what they perceive as the theological assumptions of the majority, or have been offended by the abruptness of change in the Church. They might be dissatisfied with the way the parish is doing things, or might not like some of the people in positions of prominence. The task of reconciling the alienated is a delicate one, and time is often required for wounds to heal. However, the parish leadership must make every effort to deal directly with the roots of the problem and gently integrate the alienated back into the group.

Finally, most parishes have a marginal membership made up of people who participate minimally because their level of Christian commitment is low. Although they give little priority to religion, they are not necessarily closed off entirely to the call of grace. Parish leaders certainly cannot ignore the uncommitted, but it is important to avoid pressuring them into doing what they are not yet ready to do, a temptation that is always present in a small mission parish with comparatively few members and a great many needs. Otherwise they may be pushed to the point of giving up even their minimal religious practice, and losing all contact with the Church.

The parish's uniqueness is partly determined by the fact that it has room for all these people. Members with relatively strong commitment are certainly encouraged to come together in parish groups suited to their special needs. Spiritual relationships within such groups can, in time, become quite highly developed. But *the parish as such mixes people of all levels of commitment and provides a setting in which Christians can grow and develop at different rates of speed*. That is its special contribution to the Church's life.

If a Catholic parish cannot achieve the intensity of

community possible in a covenant group, then what kind of community can it be? I would answer that it can have a moderately cohesive collective life that is at the same time functional and personal, that is based primarily on spiritual values and that, above all, is open to people from the outside.

THE FUNCTIONAL DIMENSION OF PARISH COMMUNITY

In most basic terms, Christian community implies that people routinely depend on one another for help in satisfying their ordinary, everyday spiritual needs. This means that they do things for one another not only informally and spontaneously but through stable, organized activities to which they contribute and from which they receive.

In the Church there are "gifts of ministries in which, by His own power, we serve each other unto salvation, so that carrying out the truth in love, we might through all things grow into Him who is our Head."[4] These gifts are many and varied, and include sacramental powers; skills in teaching, counseling, organizing; knowledge of Scripture, theology, liturgy and church history; time; money; pastoral servanthood; authority to foster the unity of Faith; generosity; experience of living the Christian life in the world; and many others. In the parish, all these gifts are marshalled and combined in various ways to provide structured ministries of worship (the liturgy, the Sacraments, devotions, group prayer), of teaching (CCD, adult education, religious counseling, preaching), and of support (decision-making, maintenance, administration).

---

4. Vatican II, *Dogmatic Constitution on the Church*, n. 7.

When they participate in these organized activities as ministers and/or recipients, members of the parish are expressing a functional interdependence. This interdependence can be intensified by encouraging the broadest possible participation that the demands of quality ministry and the talents, circumstances and commitment of the congregation will allow. Clearly, it is important for the parish to move beyond the point where the principal role of the laity is to passively accept the ministry of the priest. While some training will be necessary to enable laypeople to take on unfamiliar apostolic tasks, the effort is well worth it in terms of community cohesion.

THE PERSONAL DIMENSION OF PARISH COMMUNITY

A supermarket and its customers are functionally interdependent. Customers pay, the supermarket sells; cooperation in an organized activity helps put food on the table. Obviously, though, a supermarket and its customers do not form a community; community demands relationships that are not only functional, but personal as well. In the parish, priests, religious and laity must see one another not just as leaders, associates or participants in programs, but also as individuals with unique histories, personalities, feelings, talents, troubles, hopes and dreams.

On one level, Christian community demands that people working together in organized programs show personal consideration for one another. The *way* something is done is as important as the results. A parish council can function simply by making decisions. A good council, however, will take account of opposing viewpoints within the congregation before doing so. A CCD program can function if the classes meet, but in a good program the teachers will support one another and show concern for the spiritual welfare of the students. It is wrong to look upon people as mere tools for ministry; their feelings and aspirations must be allowed to shape and color parish programs. Moreover, when conflicts arise in which parishioners disagree vigorously on important issues, these disagreements must not be allowed to degenerate into hostility and personal vilification. "By this will all men know that you are my disciples, if you have love for one another" (Jn 13:35).

The leadership will sometimes have to make difficult decisions that hurt people's feelings in order to preserve the quality of a given ministry. It may be necessary, for example, to ask the finance chairman to resign if he is not doing a good job. Such situations must be handled with great kindness and sensitivity. Otherwise, the parish will be acting more like a purely utilitarian institution than a Christian community.

On a second level, the personal dimension of community finds expression in one-to-one ministry, carried out either in connection with organized programs, or informally and spontaneously. The priest and other professional church workers regularly minister to parishioners through counseling, pastoral visitation and the like. How might the laity serve one another's spiritual needs? At minimum, they should pray for one another and show a willingness to minister in a neighborly fashion as the need arises. Certainly the parish will encourage this and, for that purpose, will provide occasions for parishioners to become acquainted—not a particularly great problem in a congregation of 250 or less.

Some Catholics will go further and join prayer groups and other organizations where they explicitly commit themselves to helping fellow members grow in Christ. Because the parish is an inclusive group, however, not every parishioner can be expected to exhibit this level of concern. The individual's freedom in this matter must be respected. People should not be pressured to believe that being a good parishioner requires them to reveal their spiritual state or inner feelings, especially to persons not of their own choosing, or under circumstances that are unsuitable.

To sum up, Catholics can rightly expect certain things of their parishes: the opportunity to serve and be served through basic ministries, a style of operation that considers not only the results but the good of the people involved, and at least a minimal readiness on the part of the members to help one another out. The parish that does this has established a network of social relationships within which the individual can find ordinary spiritual nourishment and a measure of reinforcement for Christian values. The effects of sin must always be taken into account, of course. Not everyone in an inclusive community is committed and thoughtful, and disagreements do occur. No parish is perfect, even though perfection is the goal. Like every other church organization, the parish is part of a Pilgrim People.

THE SPIRITUAL BASIS OF PARISH COMMUNITY

The primary basis for parish community should be the care and concern that the members have for one ano-

ther's growth in Christ.[5] In practice, people look to the
parish for other things as well—to find friendship, to
experience a sense of belonging, or to fulfill recreational or
other important human needs. It would be absurd to ar-
gue that Christians should not be friends or should avoid
forming friendships through the medium of the parish.
The small town church has traditionally played a prominent role in the social life of the community. Parish get-
togethers provide an opportunity for members to get
acquainted, to learn cooperation under pleasant circumstances, to raise needed funds, to promote good will, and
to rejoice together in the Lord. The social dimension is
especially important in rural mission parishes in Appalachia and the South, where many of the Catholics are
newcomers to the area.

It is essential, however, that friendship, recreation and
the need to belong remain in the background. If they
were to become the *principal* reasons why people participate, the parish could lose its spiritual emphasis and
become in reality just a social club that happens to be
doing religious work. Its identity would be severely dis-
torted.

One of the consequences of a shift toward such values
would be a tendency on the congregation's part to close
itself off to outsiders. There are advantages to being part
of a small, friendly parish where everyone knows everything else, and it is easy to develop a stake in preserving
the status quo. As the group grows more cohesive, unconscious resistance to disturbing familiar, comfortable relationships can evolve, and the parish can sacrifice the

5. On the spiritual basis of parish community, see Emile Pin, "Can the
Urban Parish Be a Community?" *Gregorianum*, 41:3 (1960), p. 403.

spiritual good of potential members to a very human—and rather selfish—sense of belonging.[6]

This line of thought leads us from the first to the second part of the challenge that stands at the head of the chapter: "to make the parish the type of community that simultaneously fosters religious growth among its members and projects a sense of welcome to people on the outside." If the parish fosters religious growth in the ways I have suggested, if it becomes an inclusive community based on concern for Christian growth, it will neither consciously nor unconsciously turn away those with an interest in sharing its fellowship. Catholic families who move in from other areas will be integrated into the parish's interlocking human network without serious difficulty. Even where there is a major influx of new people, adjustments will be made to accommodate them for the Lord's sake. Perhaps most importantly, the unchurched who look in at the Christian community will see a group of individuals bound together by something stronger than social ties. They will not feel that entrance into the Church is conditional on their personal acceptability to the local group, and they will be encouraged to knock on the door.

A Community Open to All Races and Cultures

Projecting a sense of welcome is especially challenging when potential members are different in some obvious way from the body of established parishioners. In two-

6. On the other hand, there appears to be an upper limit to the size of the parish, beyond which it begins to experience all the problems inherent in large-scale organizations. See Hervé Carrier, *The Sociology of Religious Belonging* (New York: Herder and Herder, 1965), pp. 200-202. When Catholics become numerous in a given locality, the diocese often establishes a second parish.

thirds of the mission counties, a sizeable percentage of the population belongs to a distinct and self-conscious minority group—Black, Hispanic or American Indian.[7] The religious needs of these groups must be met, not only through a Christian victory over prejudice, but also through structuring the parish community in appropriate ways.[8]

Up to this point, we have assumed that the local Catholic community consisted of a single parish, or perhaps a parish and a mission with similar membership. The concept may have to be broadened when dealing with a county of mixed population. The Church does not require people to change their cultural identification as a condition for belonging. In fact, it affirms their need and desire to worship and express their religious commitment in culturally distinct ways. In pluralistic areas, therefore, the Church has often served minorities by means of particular organizational arrangements.[9] Sometimes an ethnic parish is established to which members of the minority group may belong if they wish. Another approach is for a parish to operate a mission, station, catechumenate or center specifically designed to serve them. A third ap-

7. According to the 1970 U.S. Census, mission counties contained 2,352,869 Blacks, 58,969 American Indians, and 48,010 Hispanics (the number of Hispanics is probably higher). There are 525 mission counties in which one or more of these groups constitute at least 20 percent of the population.

8. On this point, see Paul Hanley Furfey, "The Missionary Role of the Parish," in C. J. Nuesse and Thomas J. Harte, *The Sociology of the Parish* (Milwaukee: Bruce, 1951), pp. 312-314.

9. As Vatican II states: "But if . . . in certain regions, groups . . . are to be found who are kept away from embracing the Catholic Faith because they cannot adapt themselves to the peculiar form which the Church has taken on there, it is hoped that this condition will be provided for in a special way, until such time as all Christians can gather together in one community." *Decree on the Church's Missionary Activity*, n. 20.

proach is to make provision for minority people within
the larger congregation through special Masses, celebrations, organizations and activities.

No single structure is appropriate for all circumstances.
The ideal arrangement will take into account the size of
the minority group, whether its members live in clusters or
scattered throughout the county, the strength of their particular cultural identification, their desire for a special
religious setting, and the degree of contact with the dominant culture they can comfortably sustain. Unfortunately,
the ideal is not always easy to attain. The parish may lack
sufficient funds or personnel, the number of people belonging to the minority group may be very small, or members of the majority culture may be unwilling to cooperate.
Parish leaders, however, must make every effort in this
regard. Unless people strongly identified with minority
cultures are free to work out a compatible religious expression, it is hard to see how they will be able to remain
in the Church, or to join it in the first place.

If freedom requires special structural arrangements,
solidarity demands that even the appearance of unchris-
tian segregation be avoided. "There is neither Jew nor
Greek. . . . For you are all one in Christ Jesus" (Gal 3:28).
The structures of local community should in no way set up
barriers to the unity in Christ which should transcend
every human culture and style of life. This unity can be
fostered and symbolized across group lines through occasional joint worship services and cooperative ministries.
There should be easy access to the majority congregation
if individuals from the minority culture wish to make the
transition. (The Church has a responsibility to offer this
opportunity even if such cultural assimilation is opposed

by the person's own group.) Finally, if and when cultural identification among minority people weakens, or a culturally-distinct religious expression is no longer important to them, the special organizational arrangements should gradually fall into disuse, so that the local Catholic community is structurally one.

A COMMUNITY OPEN TO ALL SOCIAL CLASSES

Our nation was established in conscious reaction against the stratified societies of Europe, and the American dream is predicated in large part on the notion of social equality. We profess to believe that people can pull themselves up by their bootstraps, no matter how humble their origins. There is enough truth to this view of American society that it has endured in the popular mind, in spite of ample evidence that the dream has its limits in practice and applies more to some groups than to others. We tend to deny the existence of social class, and typically underestimate the difficulty people have in communicating across class lines.[10]

This blind spot can constitute a serious obstacle to the formation of an open and welcoming parish community. The population of most counties divides into five basic social classes—upper, upper-middle, lower-middle, upper-lower and lower—according to occupation, income, quality

10. Joseph Fichter states: "Even though the class structure exists as a concrete reality, and even though class status has immediate, personal, and objective consequences for individuals, there is still a tendency to belittle, or even ignore, its reality. What people try to believe constitutes in itself a social fact of great significance. Because of the all-pervading ideology of democracy and all that it implies, people attempt to lessen the implications and consequences of the actual stratification of categories." *Sociology* (University of Chicago Press, 1957), p. 77.

of housing, education, manners, and style of life.[11] If the
local congregation denies the reality of social class and
does not make a determined effort to expand its base, it
will tend to accommodate people from just one or two of
these groups. This phenomenon has been documented in a
number of studies.[12]

There are multiple-class parishes, but they tend to be
Sacramental centers where personal interaction is minimal. Can a parish where the members relate to one another both functionally and *personally* create the kind of
community that truly welcomes people of more than one
or two social classes? I believe so, as long as the more
deeply committed members remind themselves again and
again that God's grace transcends status barriers found
in other spheres of life, and that the ultimate unity of
parish community is to be sought in Christ. In the normal
course of events, people rarely strike up friendships with
members of different social classes, and there is no need
for them to do so simply because they belong to the same
congregation. What they *are* required to do is to associate
in organized ministries and in parish socials, to pray for
one another, and to help one another in the Lord. If
enough of the parishioners do this in a spirit of openness
and good will, the parish will succeed in forming a Eucharistic community that is not captive to a narrow social
spectrum.

11. See W. Lloyd Warner, *Social Class in America* (New York: Harper and
Row, 1960). Warner observes that a sixth—the upper-upper—is found in
some places, where the highest status is given to the oldest families in the community.

12. See, for example, W. Lloyd Warner, ed., *Yankee City* (New Haven:
Yale University Pres, 1963), pp. 189-193.

What I have said so far applies to the challenge of creating community among people whose social status ranges from upper to upper-lower class. But what about the people in the very lowest class, a sub-group whose way of life is so much at variance with that of the rest of the population that it forms a distinct culture?[13] The people I am talking about are not only poor but outcasts. When they are employed at all, their jobs are low-paying and menial. They live in tumbledown shacks and, from a middle class perspective, their households and family life are incredibly chaotic. They have little education and their children often resist attendance at school. In dress, cleanliness, manners, style of life and financial responsibility they deviate greatly from middle class standards. Unlike most Americans, the people in this group are usually not upwardly mobile. They recognize the gulf that separates them from the mainstream and rarely seek to associate with people from other backgrounds. Perhaps most importantly for our purposes, they exhibit little inclination to participate in organized activities, either in the religious or the secular spheres. The abstract thinking needed for committee work is foreign to them, and their life style is so casual that they find it nearly impossible to fulfill the

13. Everyone who has worked in mission counties has come into contact with people belonging to this group. Although no precise statistics are available, we know that they are more numerous proportionately in mission areas than in the nation as a whole. For example, 27.0 percent of adults in mission counties have completed less than five years of schooling, compared to 5.5 percent in the nation. Although all of these functional illiterates do not necessarily belong to the lowest social class, the incidence of illiteracy provides a good comparative basis for estimating the size of such a group. For a description of the people belonging to the lowest social class, see James West, *Plainville, U.S.A.* (New York: Columbia University Press, 1945), pp. 116-128.

ongoing obligations that membership in a formal group implies.

For the Church, special concern for the poor and the outcast is the very sign of Christ's presence: "Go and report to John what you have heard and seen: the blind see, the lame walk, the lepers are cleansed, . . . the poor have the gospel preached to them" (Lk 7:22). Not only must the gospel be preached but, even at the cost of great effort, the poor must be gathered into the Church. Since members of the lowest class belong in effect to a minority culture, they may require special structural arrangements. A setting for religious expression suited to their needs and outlook should be provided; this might take the form of a neighborhood mission or catechumenate, one that is informal, minimally organized and very personal. Individuals from this group who wish to play a role in the general Catholic community should, of course, be welcomed. But as long as most of them are uncomfortable in close association with other groups, they should have the option of pursuing a separate course. There is little likelihood for the present that they will be able to express their religious commitment within a parish geared to the requirements of the majority classes.

A COMMUNITY OPEN TO CATHOLICS WHO MOVE IN

A parish in a mission county must give careful attention to how Catholics moving in from outside are received. These newcomers need to be welcomed, to meet the other members of their new community, to become familiar with parish ministries, and to be included in parish activities. If they are city people, they will appreciate some help in adjusting to rural life. Assimilating them is so important for maintaining a vital community that many parishes have special committees for that purpose.[14]

Newcomers have backgrounds; they come equipped with a previous experience of Church. This can be both an advantage and a disadvantage. On the negative side, if the new arrivals have a narrow and restricted idea of the Church's mission, they may attempt to undermine some of the things the parish is trying to do. For example, the person from an urban parish who has spent years fighting to keep the parochial school open may find it difficult to see why the priorities in a rural mission setting must be so different. Time and patience should help solve this problem.

On the positive side, newcomers bring ideas and insights, fresh approaches and perspectives that can contribute strongly to the enrichment of parish life. Such ideas must be introduced gradually, even if they have great merit. A proper respect for established customs is healthy, especially in a situation where a parish must absorb a large and rapid influx of new parishioners. Haste is likely to upset parish cohesion by breeding resentment on the part of people already there.

COMMUNITY AMONG PROFESSIONAL CHURCH WORKERS

The parish that wants to retain its vigor will leave scope

---

14. Whether or not the committee approach is used, there should be some mechanism for welcoming Catholics who move into the area, those who return to religious practice after a long absence, and those who first join the Church. Moreover, the unchurched who come to Catholicism can benefit from the newly-restored catechumenate and Rite of Initiation, while those previously baptized have the new Rite of Reception into Full Communion.

for a more restricted kind of community, one that does not involve the whole congregation. As the Church's missionary history shows, priests, Sisters, Brothers and other full-time vocational workers need to form a network of relationships that the small rural parish cannot provide.[15] They need spiritual, intellectual and psychological support from their peers, both locally and in broader settings. If they lack this help, the intensity and potential of their contribution to the parish's ministry will almost inevitably suffer.

Vocational church workers can gain some support from participation in the life of the diocese, religious congregations, lay institutes and covenant groups, as well as from retreats and educational programs. But this is not enough. What church workers need most of all is regular support at home, both in their ministry and in their personal lives. This continuing support normally comes from association among peers working in a single parish or a cluster of neighboring parishes.[16] It may take the form of a team ministry whose purpose is cooperation in the apostolate, personal spiritual enrichment, or a combination of both.[17] Team ministry is traditional in the Church's missionary life, and its restoration in our time is a sign of new and serious missionary commitment. When a group of dedicated Christians pool their talents

15. With rare exceptions, missionaries have not been sent out alone. See, for example, Joseph Masson, *Histoire universelle des missions catholiques*, Vol. 4 (Paris:Librairie Grund, 1958), pp. 123 ff.

16. See "The Support Emphasis" in David Byers, *New Directions for the Rural Church* (New York: Paulist Press, 1978), pp. 45 ff.

17. A discussion of the issues facing rural team ministries will be found in David Byers, *The Pastoral Ministry Program in the Diocese of Grand Island* (Washington, D.C.: Glenmary Research Center, 1976).

and enthusiasm, they create a healthy atmosphere in which to overcome their difficulties and get on with the Lord's work.[18]

Challenge 2

SEEKING CHRIST FIRST

To place Christ rather than institutional well-being at the center of parish community life

Years ago, I was privileged to start a parish in an area the Church had never before attempted to serve. There were only a few Catholics at first—barely a congregation. We met for Mass in a borrowed hall and all our ministries, except those connected with the liturgy, were in the future. I can clearly remember wondering by what miracle the Lord intended to mold this band of faithful people into a Christian community.

After a time our parish started to grow, and we began to organize our ministries. Our experience was not at all unusual. Within the first year, any parish with more than a handful of families will require a structure for its Christian education program. Providing a place for worship demands a budget, so there must be some means of raising

18. In working out the practical arrangements for a team ministry, however, those involved should bear in mind that, in most rural communities, a resident priest is a powerful symbol of the Church's presence. It is true that priests living together in a central town can serve the Sacramental needs of Catholics scattered over a wide area. They can be much more effective in their ministry to the community at large, however, if they reside in as many locations as possible, even if they must live alone.

funds. Before too long, the need to make decisions and plan as a community will call forth something like a parish council. No group can exist without organizational (institutional) elements.

The crucial problem is not just to develop an organization, but to develop it in a Christian context. A vital Catholic parish will *have* an organization, but it cannot be *defined* as one. Through baptism, its members have received a share in the divine life. As a fellowship of the baptized, the parish is a community whose members should be in living relationship to God and to one another. Its group life must have an inner radiance, a gospel quality, a spiritual center. As the parish matures and the organizational elements become more complex, the pastor and people must keep the structure from occupying center stage, from hardening, from becoming an obstacle to the change demanded by an evolving vision of what the parish is supposed to do and be. Otherwise there is danger that the parish will become *just* another organization, in spite of its religious activities.

THE INVISIBLE DIMENSION

God is at work in the world, both in the human heart and in human history as a whole. The parish is a tool, a crude one perhaps, in this divine work of salvation because it has pleased God "to make people holy and save them not merely as individuals without any mutual bonds, but by making them into a single people, which acknowledges Him in truth and serves Him in holiness."[19] Faith en-

19. Vatican II, *Dogmatic Constitution on the Church*, n. 9.

ables the parish to remember that it is doing the Lord's work. The leadership, clerical and lay, has a responsibility to nourish this faith, and to project such a concrete awareness of spiritual realities that the parish will always see itself as it truly is—firmly rooted in one world, nourished by another.

Because it is doing the Lord's work, the parish is dependent on the Lord's power, and cannot boast when its activities bear fruit. The good that it does, the spiritual change it fosters in people, are gifts that no purely human effort could produce. Nevertheless, since ministry operates on two levels simultaneously, the human effort is essential. The parish must bring every talent it can muster to its everyday ministry; as in the Eucharist, the Lord blesses the work of human hands.

When the parish sins, either through laziness or lack of trust, its members must collectively ask forgiveness. Each time they do so, they will be reminded once again of their pilgrim status as servants of other pilgrims in the time between the times. And when the parish ministers, its members must be conscious that grace is working not only in their own hearts, but also in the hearts of those they serve. In God's marvelous plan, they receive His gift from others as they offer His gifts to them. Their ministry, both inside and outside the Catholic community, implies a true exchange.

SEEKING CHRIST IN PRAYER

Although Christians will pray to the Father in secret (Mt 6:6), they need the support and encouragement that community prayer provides. The liturgy, especially the Eucharist, is the center and culmination of the whole life of the parish community, the "summit toward which the activity of the Church is directed, ... the fountain from which all her power flows."[20] In the Eucharist, the parishioners offer themselves to God: "For all their works, prayers, and apostolic endeavors, their ordinary married and family life, their daily occupations, their physical and mental relaxation, if carried out in the Spirit, and even the hardships of life, if patiently borne—all these become spiritual sacrifices acceptable to God through Jesus Christ. Together with the offering of the Lord's body, they are most fittingly offered in the celebration of the Eucharist."[21] By participating in the common sacrificial meal, the members of the parish enter into the paschal mystery more deeply, and "thus become a firmly-knit body in the unity of the charity of Christ"[22] The vital spirit of the Catholic community takes flame from the Eucharist and radiates outward to the community at large.

The parish also provides the other Sacraments, the Church's blessings, penitential practices, devotions, days of recollection, the celebration of feasts and seasons, and the opportunity to pray in small groups. From time to time it arranges for members of the parish to participate in spiritual exercises which intensify their religious commitment: missions, retreats, Cursillos, Search Programs,

20. Vatican II, *Constitution on the Sacred Liturgy*, n. 10. See also Vatican II, *Dogmatic Constitution on the Church*, (n. 11): "Taking part in the Eucharistic Sacrifice, which is the font and apex of the whole Christian life, [the faithful] offer the Divine Victim to God, and offer themselves along with It."
21. Vatican II, *Dogmatic Constitution on the Church*, n. 34.
22. Vatican II, *Decree on the Bishops' Pastoral Office in the Church*, n. 15.

Marriage Encounters, and similar activities. These events and programs, usually conducted by people from the outside, offer peak experiences that can free parishioners momentarily from the grip of secular interests, strengthen their spiritual lives, and make it easier for them to seek the things that are above (Col 3:1). Invigorated by a fresh perspective, they grow more sensitive to their Christian responsibilities, both in the parish and in the world.

By calling parishioners to pray together, the parish brings them into closer relationship with the Lord and one another. But the congregation will not become Christ-centered merely because its members are prayerful people. Prayer must also penetrate the organizational life of the parish, becoming part of everything it does as a group.

Prayer is especially important to the parish council. The way a congregation develops—quickly or slowly, for good or for ill—reflects the wisdom of the decisions it takes month by month and year by year. *The principal responsibility of the parish council is to seek to know the Lord's will for the community at any given time.* While it must consider hard, practical facts in choosing a course of action, the decision to adopt one alternative and reject another is ultimately a value judgment to be made under the guidance of the Spirit. It is essential, therefore, that the members pray together over the matters before them. This prayer must be an integral part of the decision-making process, not a token observance crammed into five minutes at the beginning or end of the meeting. Otherwise there is real danger that the parish, in performing its group functions, will lose sight of those spiritual values which justify its existence.

SEEKING CHRIST IN FAITH

"Faith then depends on hearing, and hearing on the word of Christ" (Rom 10:17). In the parish celebration of the Eucharist and other liturgical settings, preaching communicates God's power to those who believe. In parish educational programs for adults and children, instruction reveals "the whole mystery of Christ . . . , those truths the ignorance of which is ignorance of Christ."[23]

Once accepted, the word of God is a two-edged sword, both a comfort and a challenge. The parish preaches a gospel which ennobles, which eases the burdens of life. But that same gospel disturbs, intrudes on human consciousness, challenges secular assumptions, and demands that people make difficult individual and collective choices. The scriptural Christ the parish proclaims in word and deed is not fashioned according to contemporary American ideals and values, but according to the faith of the universal Church. Because the parish is in communion with this faith through the offices of the pastor and the bishop, its teaching liberates. It helps parishioners transcend their own culture and experience in addressing the all-important gospel question, "What think you of Christ?"

SHARING THE CROSS AND RESURRECTION

Since the parish has a spiritual dimension, its triumphs and tragedies are not just organizational successes and failures. Just as the individual Christian is called to enter

23. *Ibid.*, n. 12.

personally into the paschal mystery, the parish is called to share in the death and resurrection of the Lord. Sometimes the cross comes from outside the congregation and sometimes from within. The parish may experience hostility, for example, because it espouses urgent but unpopular causes. People may be indifferent to its ministry, or reject it by exercising their freedom to say no. Dissension within the congregation can cause intense pain to those who want the parish to be the sort of community in which Christians really do love one another.

Through all these crises, and through the happy times when all wounds are temporarily healed, the parish must remember that its life has a recurring pulse: death and renewal, the cross and the tomb and the glorious resurrection. Accepted in a spirit of faith, all these experiences help detach the parish from institutional self-seeking, and enable it to advance in Christian commitment more than it falls back.

Challenge 3

CATHOLIC IDENTITY

To preserve and strengthen the Catholic identity of parishioners, who constitute a religious minority in mission areas

In areas of the country where Catholicism is strong and pervasive, a number of factors converge to help people retain and deepen their sense of identification with the

Church. In the typical Catholic family, both parents will be Catholic, not just one. Many of the people that Catholics rub shoulders with on the job, in civic activities and in social life share their religious beliefs. Parishioners are surrounded by the institutional evidence of Catholic commitment: churches, hospitals, colleges, social service agencies, priests and religious.[24] Diocesan liturgical celebrations provide a means of expressing solidarity with the Church at large. Parochial schools offer not only systematic religious instruction, but also the opportunity for enculturation in the Catholic tradition.[25] Mass, the Sacraments, religious education, pastoral care, retreats, social programs and other ministries are readily available, and in such profusion that people often have alternatives to choose from in satisfying their religious needs.

Not all the influences in heavily Catholic areas are positive, of course. The surrounding culture is hostile or indifferent to values like self-denial, the unity of marriage and the right to life. The humanistic and materialistic behavior appealingly displayed in movies, on television and in advertisements can erode standards without directly attacking them. In the Church itself there is scandal, sin, rigidity, dissension, and the impersonal formalism that sometimes invades religious institutions when they attempt to serve large numbers of people. For these and other reasons, many fail to internalize their religion, re-

24. Philip J. Murnion, "The Parish as Source of Community and Identity," in Evelyn Whitehead, ed., *The Parish in Community and Ministry* (New York: Paulist Press, 1978), pp. 101 ff.

25. See Andrew M. Greeley and Peter H. Rossi, *Education of Catholic Americans* (Chicago: Aldine, 1966). See also David Elkind, "The Child's Conception of His Religious Denomination: The Catholic Child," *The Journal of Genetic Psychology*, 101 (1962), 185-193.

maining lukewarm in religious practice or drifting away from the Church altogether.[26] On balance, however, Catholic areas do provide a setting generally favorable to the development of an authentic Catholic religious spirit.

By way of contrast, mission areas offer little support for Catholic identity.[27] Catholics in such areas are subject to the same materialistic influences as are found everywhere else. Moreover, they lack the reinforcement that comes from general association with people of their own religious tradition. They are members of a religious minority that often amounts to less than one percent of the local population, and they live among other Christians who, though generally ecumenically-minded, disagree with many Catholic teachings. It is easy to lose perspective in such a setting. Social pressure alone is enough to breed indifferentism in religious matters; the individual wants to fit in, to be accepted. People newly-arrived from heavily Catholic areas carry some immunity to these pressures, but it does not last forever. Their children and grandchildren will never have this immunity at all; they must build identification with the Church on different foundations.

In rural mission areas, the task of developing Catholic identity falls squarely on the parish, since it is usually the only formal expression of the Church's presence. The parish must take this responsibility seriously. Unless the parishioners have such a strong sense of loyalty to the uni-

26. See J. Russell Hale, *Who Are the Unchurched?* (Washington, D.C.: Glenmary Research Center, 1977); *The Unchurched American* (Princeton, N.J.: The Gallup Organization, 1978).

27. For a discussion of identity among marginal groups, see Hans J. Mol, *Identity and the Sacred* (New York: Free Press, 1976), pp. 31 ff.

versal Catholic experience of Christianity that Catholicism becomes a central element in their self-definition, it is hard to see how the Faith will ever be firmly planted in this new ground.

The parish cannot succeed by building a psychological wall around its members to shield them from alien religious contacts. Anyone who reached adulthood by the 1950's will remember the days when Catholics rarely associated with Protestants on a religious level, although the two groups mingled freely enough in secular life. Invisible boundaries were created around the parish, internally by fear of indifferentism and externally by conscious or unconscious opposition. Today the conscious opposition has all but disappeared and Christians of many communions, including Catholics, are seeking to know and learn from one another, laying the groundwork for a common witness. Whatever ways the parish uses to foster Catholic identity must take the ecumenical spirit into account. The social boundaries that formerly isolated Christian groups from one another have no place in today's world.[28]

How, then, can the parish approach identity formation? Before addressing that question, I must say something about the nature of Catholic identity itself. *Authentic identity does not mean cultural Catholicism unsupported by inner convictions. It implies the possession of a personal value system that is not only Catholic in content but mature in development as well.*

28. For example, Vatican II states: "Before the whole world let all Christians confess their faith in God, one and three, in the incarnate Son of God, our Redeemer and Lord. United in their efforts, and with mutual respect, let them bear witness to our common hope which does not play us false." *Decree on Ecumenism*, n. 12.

A value system is a complex of organized thinking, feeling and willing in accordance with which a person is habitually disposed to act. A mature religious value system has certain characteristics.[29] First of all, it is *comprehensive*—it takes in everything central to existence as a human being. No area is excluded. It is capable of interpreting every reality that can come within the horizon of experience and, further, of offering a clue to the ultimate meaning of life.

Second, in accordance with the nature of reality itself, the mature value system is *rich and complex*. Mature people do not make judgments based on simplistic abstractions. While they may recognize and even cherish the ideal notion of love, for example, they must be able to break that notion down into its component parts, developing an emotional-rational attitude towards each of its major applications to life. They do not accept a slice of reality for the whole—seeing the potential for good in people, say, while ignoring their potential for evil. Nor do they seize on one or two beliefs uncritically and uphold them with fanatical intensity to the exclusion of all others.

Third, the various parts of a mature value system are in *harmonious balance*. They are welded together into a logical consistency, not left rattling about in the mind like an odd assortment of hubcaps in a junkyard. No system will be completely harmonious, of course, but maturity implies a continuing commitment to struggling with the major dilemmas of religious thought—the relationship of grace to free will, for example, or the problem of evil.

29. For a more extended discussion of the points outlined here, see Gordon W. Allport, *The Individual and His Religion* (New York: Macmillan, 1950), pp. 52-74.

Fourth, someone with a mature value system will be *re-flective*, always relating new ideas, new facts, new experiences to the system as a whole. Such an individual will never consciously sweep a disturbing conceptual crumb under the rug. Only by ever broadening the inner synthesis can people remain in dialogue with the flow of life, and prevent their religion from becoming peripheral to the personality or shriveling into an escape mechanism.

Fifth, a mature religious value system *influences behavior*; it moves the individual to judge and to act. Even mature people sin; conscience points one way and they hurry off in another. But their value system provides a standard by which they measure the moral quality of conduct, and prompts the steps they take in light of this judgment.

Sixth, a person with a mature value system rises above self-fulfillment and achieves *self-transcendence*. The religious impulse is related to the quest for what is viewed as good: food, clothing, shelter, security, comfort, health, self-expression, accomplishment, self-esteem, prestige, emotional experience, belonging, pleasure, love, beauty and knowledge. A child's religion is self-centered, with special reference to organic desires. As life goes on, however, suffering and deprivation can force a shift in perspective. Depending on the quality of the response to these realities, people can gradually abandon the idea of self-fulfillment and become open to the world of the sacred— the "totally other" which is outside and beyond. At this point, the value system is no longer centered on those objects, mental and physical, that produce pleasure, pain, joy and sorrow. They are relegated (not without effort) to their proper but subordinate role. The overwhelming value becomes not personal needs, of whatever order, but service and dedication to God and others.[30]

It is the parish's responsibility to help people achieve Catholic identity by developing this comprehensive, complex, harmonious, reflective, action-oriented, transcendent value system based on the Church's witness to the resurrection, two thousand years of tradition and a worldwide Faith. Identity is created and reinforced through certain avenues: association with the like-minded, the acting out of convictions, the celebration of values and reflective knowledge. To be successful, then, the parish must be able to communicate the value system by means of these channels. It must establish a powerful Catholic presence in the lives of those it seeks to form.

ASSOCIATION

In daily life, parishioners participate in a number of reference groups: family, kinship, occupational, school, recreational, friendship, civic and religious. Such participation has an impact for good or for ill on religious values.[31] Generally speaking, the strength of the impact will vary with the importance one attaches to a particular group; this is especially true for primary groups, those characterized by frequent, face-to-face highly personal interaction. Different reference groups are likely to be dominant at different stages of life. The family has an overwhelming influence on young children, for exam-

30. See William Ashdown, *Motivation and Response in Religion* (Washington, D.C.: Glenmary Research Center, 1972), pp. 139-143.
31. See Muzafer Sherif, "Self Concept," in the *International Encyclopedia of the Social Sciences*, and "Ego-Involvements and Reference Groups," in *An Outline of Social Psychology* (New York: Harper, 1956), pp. 619-647.

ple, while the collective judgment of the peer group is frequently decisive during adolescence.[32]

The parish does not enjoy direct access to every group in which its people are active; indeed, it may be completely closed off from some that have a significant effect on identity formation. As noted earlier, this constitutes one of the principal differences between living in a community where Catholicism is strong and living where it is a minority religion. The parish does, however, have several avenues of approach. As a Eucharistic community, it is itself a group. It can also create sub-units within the parish structure, and some of these can be of a primary nature: prayer groups, committees, and so on. It can encourage people to associate with other Catholics at the diocesan or regional level. Finally and most importantly, the parish is in a position to strongly influence family life.

Let us examine these possibilities more closely. To the extent that the parish is a community of brothers and sisters in Christ, parishioners can confirm their Catholic values by observing them reflected in one another. The support one can derive from this general association is rarely adequate, however; most parishes contain a number of people with only minimal Catholic commitment. This is where the small primary sub-groups can be useful. They can offer their members a degree of reinforcement unavailable from the congregation at large. I realize that some mission parishes have so few people that

32. See Raymond G. Carey, "The Influence of Peers in Shaping Religious Behavior," *Journal for the Scientific Study of Religion*, 10 (1971), 157-159. See also Erik H. Erikson, *Identity, Youth and Crisis* (New York: Norton, 1968), pp. 91 ff.

creating these small groups is impractical. But that does not diminish their importance for fostering religious development; they remain a future option.

Any parish, no matter how small, can promote participation in diocesan and regional Catholic organizations. Distance, of course, creates a problem in rural areas, placing unavoidable limitations on such participation. Yet in terms of fostering Catholic identity, taking advantage of opportunities to meet and work with people from other places—especially other rural mission parishes—is well worth the effort.

Through relationships within the family, children absorb the values of their parents, and husbands and wives learn by observing their children and each other.[33] The family generates a set of attitudes and an orientation that color all of reality; more than any other social institution, it helps shape the individual's response to religion and the Church. Whatever the parish can do to instill a Christian spirit in family life, therefore, is bound to have significant impact on people's sense of Catholic identity.

Once again, there is a special circumstance to be considered in mission counties. The task of fostering a specifically Catholic identity in children can be complicated by the typically high number of mixed marriages. Experience shows, however, that non-Catholic parents often appreciate the opportunity to take part in Catholic family programs, even if they themselves have no intention of joining the Church.

---

33. See Hervé Carrier, *The Sociology of Religious Belonging* (New York: Herder and Herder, 1965), pp. 117-130.

BEHAVIOR

The most effective way to achieve and maintain a solid Catholic identity is to live out the two greatest commandments, worshipping God and serving others.[34] "My dear children, let us not love in word, neither with the tongue, but in deed and in truth" (1 Jn 3:18). An individual attains self-transcendence by behaving like a self-transcendent person, and by taking care to refine and purify the underlying motivation. The parish should be a classroom where people learn by doing. Besides offering encouragement to individual initiative, it should give parishioners the chance to participate in organized programs that help their neighbors. To the extent that the parish gets its members to do things, and to do them for the right reasons, it is fostering the development of their religious values.

While all unselfish behavior enhances religious maturation, the ministry of evangelization has a special worth. A person learns to identify with the Catholic Faith by trying to share that Faith with others. Preaching the gospel not only expresses a commitment but strengthens it as well. Teaching something to others makes me teach it to myself.

CELEBRATION

Identity is also reinforced through public celebration of Catholic values.[35] The parish stands at the center of Christian ritual. It is the setting for the daily and weekly

---

34. Carrier, p. 112.
35. Carrier, pp. 110 ff; Mol, pp. 233 ff.

Mass, the observation of the feasts and seasons, the Sacrament of Reconciliation, and the symbolic expressions of faith that mark the major passages of life: birth, growth, marriage, vocation and entry into the world beyond. Whenever people come together to thank the Lord and enjoy His gifts, to beg His forgiveness or to ask for comfort in sorrow, they are confirmed in the Faith they have been granted.

The office of bishop is the symbolic embodiment of communion with the Chair of Peter and the universal Church; and "... in the bishop, ... Our Lord Jesus Christ, the Supreme High Priest, is present in the midst of those who believe."[36] The parish should seize every opportunity to promote a sense of solidarity with the diocese, especially through personal contact with the bishop and participation with him in the Eucharist and other celebrations.

REFLECTION

One of the ways education liberates is by enabling us to see beyond the horizons our culture imposes. In mission areas, parish educational programs are the principal means for bringing people into contact with the great Catholic ideas and traditions that form part of a worldwide expression of religious faith.[37] The pastor and other vocational missioners, whose extended training has familiarized them with Catholic history and thought, should make every effort to see that the members of the con-

36. Vatican II, *Dogmatic Constitution on the Church*, n. 21.
37. For an expansion of this point, see Romano Guardini, "The Church, Encounter with Christ," in *The Church* (New York: Kenedy, 1963), pp. 16-29.

gregation are exposed to the teaching of the Church as past generations have lived it, and as it is now expressed in unity and diversity within many nations and cultures.

This education must keep pace with the parishioners' own growth in age and religious sophistication. So as to foster a truly mature value system, parish instruction will gradually become more complex (treating, for example, not only the achievements of Catholicism, but also its historical inadequacies), more comprehensive (covering all matters central to existence), and more balanced (showing how the parts fit into the whole). Finally, the parish will help its members to relate their beliefs to the realities they encounter in their everyday lives.

This last element is particularly important for fostering Catholic identity. It is not enough to teach people things; at least the same amount of effort must go towards helping them integrate their religious knowledge with their experience. The parish must encourage such practical application in two spheres. First, people must learn to judge the values prevalent in American culture by comparing them with gospel values. There are many ways of doing this, either as part of the Christian education program or in connection with other parish activities. In one rural parish the pastor invited two or three families to join him in watching a certain movie on television. When it was over, the group discussed the values of the principal characters and the degree of sympathy with which these values were set forth. The commercials were treated the same way. People were a little surprised to discover, when they thought about it, that they had been placidly accepting things on television that were not very Christian. Even the heroes, for example, had the habit of provoking confrontations and then shooting or punching their opponents. After contrasing Christian values with movie morality on several occasions, the families began to develop a critical faculty that carried over into real life. They became much more conscious of their Catholic beliefs and realized that, as Christians, they are often called upon to reject values that American culture generally approves.

Second, parishioners should be trained to view the Church's teaching against the backdrop of the majority religions in the area. It is inconceivable that someone could develop a sound Catholic identity without reflecting on the principal differences between Catholicism and other Christian Faiths, especially when these Faiths have helped shape the local culture. Such reflection, of course, cannot be undertaken in a spirit of triumphalism or competition; it would be absurd to compare Catholic ideals with Protestant lapses. On the contrary, the parishioners should learn to appreciate other traditions and to recognize the practical shortcomings of their own. Objective and generous analysis will not prevent Catholics from feeling a deep sense of loyalty and enthusiasm for the unique gifts they possess as members of a religion that has touched so many hearts in so many ages and places. Without such enthusiasm, in fact, true Catholic identity can never be achieved.

Challenge 4

CHRISTIAN UNITY

To promote unity among all Christians

It is the task of the local congregation not only to nourish the spiritual life of its members, however important that may be, but also to reach out to the community at large. In mission areas, a substantial proportion of that outreach will consist in efforts to promote Christian unity, simply because the majority of people who live there happen to be members of non-Catholic Churches and Ecclesial Communions.

In discerning the signs of the times, Vatican II strongly affirmed the urgency of this task: "Many Christian communions present themselves . . . as the true inheritors of Jesus Christ; all indeed profess to be followers of the Lord but they differ in mind and go their different ways, as if Christ Himself were divided. Certainly, such division openly contradicts the will of Christ, scandalizes the world, and damages that most holy cause, the preaching of the gospel to every creature."[38] The Council Fathers also reminded Catholics that in seeking unity with other Christians they receive as well as give: "Nor should we forget that anything wrought by the grace of the Holy Spirit in the hearts of our separated brethren can contribute to our own edification. Whatever is truly Christian is never contrary to what genuinely belongs to the faith; indeed, it can always bring a more perfect realization of

---

38. Vatican II, *Decree on Ecumenism*, n. 1.

the very mystery of Christ and the Church."[39] The search for unity, therefore, implies a true exchange. By sharing God's gifts with one another, we affirm our common beliefs and grow together in Christ. Step by step we move toward that unity to which the Lord is calling us and which, at this moment in history, our honest differences will permit.

This concern for Christian unity involves the Church at every level: international, national, diocesan and local.[40] Parish ecumenism is important; it has its own proper role, dynamics, needs and resources. In fact, without parish ecumenism, carried out in accordance with diocesan policies and under the bishop's guidance, efforts at other levels have little chance of success.[41]

INDIRECT ECUMENISM

Much of what the parish does to advance Christian unity is a by-product of activities that have something else as their immediate goal. For example, when the parish promotes *religious development* and interior conversion among its own members and works to make its group life

---

39. *Ibid.*, n. 4.

40. Vatican II states: "The concern for restoring unity involves the whole Church, faithful and clergy alike." *Decree on Ecumenism*, n. 9.

41. The Secretariat for Promoting Christian Unity states: "Ecumenism on the local level is a primary element of the ecumenical situation as a whole. It is not secondary nor merely derivative. It faces specific needs and situations and has its own resources. It has an initiative of its own and its task is a wider one than merely implementing world-wide ecumenical directives on a small scale." *Ecumenical Collaboration at the Regional, National and Local Levels* (Washington, D.C.: National Conference of Catholic Bishops, 1975), p. 6. This document sets out "orientations which do not have the force of law but which have the weight of the experience and insights of the Secretariat."

truly Christian, it is creating an atmosphere in which ecumenism can flourish. The closer our union with the Father, the Son and the Holy Spirit, the more readily we open ourselves to our non-Catholic neighbors.[42] *Practical cooperation* among congregations can also contribute powerfully to a sense of oneness in Christ. A coalition of local churches can be formed to help the poor and address urgent social problems.[43] Catholics and Protestants can explore possibilities for common witness to the unchurched, to the extent that present theological differences will permit.[44] Congregations can even cooperate in certain aspects of the pastoral ministry, to the benefit of all.[45] Such joint efforts might include coordinating

42. Vatican II, *Decree on Ecumenism*, nn. 6-7.

43. For examples of such collaboration, see Secretariat for Christian Unity, *Ecumenical Collaboration*, p. 14.

44. Pope Paul VI states: "We make our own the desire of the Fathers of the Third General Assembly of the Synod of Bishops, for a collaboration marked by greater commitment with the Christian brethren with whom we are not yet united in perfect unity, taking as a basis the foundation of Baptism and the patrimony of faith which is common to us. By doing this we can already give a greater common witness to Christ before the world in the very work of evangelization. Christ's command urges us to do this; the duty of preaching and of giving witness to the gospel requires this." *Apostolic Exhortation on Evangelization in the Modern World*, n. 77. Vatican II states: "Insofar as religious conditions allow, ecumenical activity should be furthered in such a way that, excluding any appearance of indifference or confusion on the one hand, or of unhealthy rivalry on the other, Catholics should cooperate in a brotherly spirit with their separated brethren, according to the norms of the *Decree on Ecumenism*, making before the nations a common profession of faith, insofar as their beliefs are common, in God and in Jesus Christ, and cooperating in social and in technical projects as well as in cultural and religious ones. Let them cooperate especially for the sake of Christ, their common Lord: let His Name be the bond that unites them! This cooperation should be undertaken not only among private persons, but also, subject to approval by the local Ordinary, among churches or ecclesial communities and their works." *Decree on Ecumenism*, n. 15.

45. See Secretariat for Christian Unity, *Ecumenical Collaboration*, pp. 10 ff.

chaplain services in jails and hospitals so that Christians of different denominations have ready access to their proper pastors; supplementing regular catechesis with ecumenical lectures or courses on noncontroversial topics; and sharing facilities, either on a regular basis or for specified activities.[46]

DIRECT ECUMENISM

Besides promoting ecumenism indirectly, parishes must take steps deliberately aimed at bringing Christians together. The first task is to break down prejudice, to promote good will across denominational lines, and to help Catholics and other Christians become comfortable with one another in a religious setting. Given the modern interest in ecumenism and the neighborly quality of small

---

46. The Secretariat for Christian Unity states: "In hospitals the chaplains often adopt an ecumenical approach, both for some of their contacts with the patients and for their dealings with the hospital authorities." *Ecumenical Collaboration*, p. 10. With reference to catechesis, the Secretariat states: "In catechetics local needs have led at times to collaboration in the teaching of religion, especially where this has to be done in non-denominational schools. But as long as Christians are not fully at one in faith, catechesis, which is formation for profession of faith, must remain necessarily the proper and inalienable task of the various churches and ecclesial communities." *Ecumenical Collaboration*, p. 13. And with reference to shared facilities: "The rule is that Catholic churches are reserved for Catholic worship. As consecrated buildings they have an important liturgical significance. Further they have a pedagogical value for inculcating the meaning and spirit of worship. Therefore sharing them with other Christians or constructing new churches jointly with other Christians can be only by way of exception." Examples of cases in which bishops may permit exceptions are: (1) the separated brethren have no place in which to carry out their religious rites; (2) a need or emergency; and (3) chapels in airports or military camps. *Ecumenical Collaboration*, p. 11. See also Secretariat for Promoting Christian Unity, *Directory for the Application of the Decisions of the Second Ecumenical Council of the Vatican Concerning Ecumenical Matters*, Part I (May 14, 1967), nn. 29 and 61.

town life, a general *spirit of friendliness* is not very difficult to achieve. Catholic pastors and parish leaders can open communication with their counterparts in other congregations, and can respond warmly to overtures from the outside. In doing so they must, of course, be aware of the limits to ecumenical involvement that their own and other Churches impose. To act otherwise is to raise false expectations and risk doing more harm than good. They must also be sensitive to the feelings of people on both sides of the denominational fence and allow room for adjustment, without demanding too much all at once.

When the time is right, the parish can begin to *establish contact* in a specifically religious setting. This contact may take the form of meetings where the members of different Churches become acquainted or discuss a topic of mutual interest. Or the Catholics may exchange visits with another congregation, the visitors observing the worship service of their hosts, listening to a brief talk by one or both pastors, perhaps taking part in a coffee hour or potluck supper. Feelers of this sort often prepare the way for the practical cooperation I discussed above. Their primary value, however, lies in setting the stage for ecumenism at a deeper and more comprehensive level.[47]

If ecumenical efforts are to succeed, sooner or later they must go beyond friendly association to *prayer for unity*. "In humble prayer we beg pardon of God and of our separated brethren [for sins against unity], just as we forgive them that offend us."[48] And we pray with our Lord

---

47. See Secretariat for Promoting Christian Unity, *Reflections and Suggestions Concerning Ecumenical Dialogue* (Washington, D.C.: National Conference of Catholic Bishops, 1970), p. 10.

48. Vatican II, *Decree on Ecumenism*, n. 7.

"that all may be one, even as thou, Father, in me and I in thee; that they also may be one in us, that the world may believe that thou hast sent me" (Jn 17:21). Some of this prayer will take place in the parish itself, at Mass and on other occasions. But Catholic congregations should also join in common prayer with Protestant Churches "in a manner and to a degree permissible and appropriate in [Christianity's] present divided state."[49] Prayer services for unity and other common concerns may be held. The people may pray together during ecumenical meetings or while carrying out cooperative projects. They may even participate in liturgical worship with non-Catholics from time to time, according to the norms of church law.[50] Besides calling down God's grace, this common prayer symbolizes the unity we now have, and awakens a sense of longing for the day when differences will be overcome. (In addition to what it does as a community, of course, the parish can encourage those members who are mature in faith and secure in their Catholic identity to participate as individuals in ecumenical prayer meetings, retreats, and the like.)

While prayer is essential for promoting unity, it must be supported by understanding and communication among Christian groups. This requires instruction and dialogue. Parishioners need to know that other Christians represent a variety of religious traditions and cannot be simply lumped together as "Protestants." They need at least elementary *instruction* in the history, spiritual ideals, organization, beliefs and prayer life of the area's principal

49. Secretariat for Christian Unity, *Directory*, Part I, n. 25.
50. *Ibid.*, nn. 32-63.

denominations.[51] There is a clear value to inviting representatives of other Faiths—pastors, theologians, congregational leaders—to contribute to this instruction. But
the primary responsibility for interpreting the outlook
of non-Catholics in Catholic terms falls to the pastor and
those who aid him in conducting the parish's religious
education program. They have the knowledge to clarify
what the Catholic Church and various Protestant
Churches hold in common and where the principal differences lie. We must hope that they will also have the
tact to create an atmosphere of respect and appreciation
for God's gifts to others, and the intellectual discipline to
avoid a spirit of "doctrinal indifferentism, which would
claim that, before the mystery of Christ and the Church,
all positions are equivalent."[52]

As the ecumenical climate in the county improves, the
time will come when the Catholic parish and one or more
Protestant congregations feel the desire for serious, substantial and regular religious contact. Each congregation
will want to grow in appreciation of the other's tradition;
to explore the practical challenges and problems that face
the Christian, whether Protestant or Catholic; to gain a
clear perception of what unites them and awaken a sense
of sorrow over what still divides. These goals are achieved
through *ecumenical dialogue* in the strict sense, where

51. Vatican II states: "We must get to know the outlook of our separated
brethren. Study is absolutely required for this, and it should be pursued in fi-
delity to truth and with a spirit of good will. Catholics who already have a proper grounding, need to acquire a more adequate understanding of the respective
doctrines of our separated brethren, their history, their spiritual and liturgical
life, their religious psychology and cultural background." *Decree on Ecumenism*,
n. 9.

52. Secretariat for Christian Unity, *Reflections and Suggestions*, p. 10.

representatives of different traditions meet on an equal footing "to listen and reply, to understand and to be understood, to pose questions and to be questioned in turn."[53] It goes without saying that this dialogue should not degenerate into polemic; the positions the participating Churches take on issues should be stated "in a constructive manner, putting aside the tendency to define by opposition."[54] On the other hand, "nothing is so foreign to the spirit of ecumenism as a false irenicism which harms the purity of Catholic doctrine and obscures its true and genuine meaning."[55]

Advance preparation is important. Relatively few of the people who take part in ecumenical dialogue at the parish level will have professional theological training, yet they may find themselves examining some complex matters. The topic for discussion should be announced well ahead of time, so that the members of each congregation, individually and collectively, can prepare themselves by adequate study and reflection.[56]

The small rural parish is not expected, of course, to develop ties to every denomination in the county all at once. What can be done will be limited by time and energy, and by the attitudes toward ecumenism that prevail in the other churches. From the beginning, however, the parish can do its part to create a climate of friendliness and cooperation. Through the years, it can provide instruction for Catholics about the history and beliefs of

---

53. *Ibid.*, p. 6.
54. *Ibid.*, p. 16.
55. Vatican II, *Decree on Ecumenism*, n. 11.
56. For additional details, see Secretariat for Christian Unity, *Reflections and Suggestions*, pp. 11-13.

other Communions. It can gradually establish initial religious contact with a number of groups, and can pray for unity, both by itself and together with other Christians. It can work toward establishing dialogue with one or more non-Catholic congregations, and can even consider a covenant relationship with one of them that involves a mutual pledge to engage in ecumenical activities in certain specified ways.

In all this, the parish will not overlook establishing communication with at least some denominations whose worship and congregational life are informal, and very much different from our own. In addition, it will try to relate not only to denominations already deeply committed to ecumenism, but to those that tend to hold back. This is especially important when the less ecumenically-minded groups constitute the majority religions of the area. Although it is suitable and necessary for the Catholic congregation to talk to other small churches, the scandal of division on the local scene will persist unless the predominant faiths are also brought into the discussion.

Reconciling Individuals

Until now, I have been discussing an approach to Christian unity that is strictly ecumenical—that is, Church-to-Church. But individual baptized Christians can also achieve unity with the Catholic Church through personal profession of faith. Vatican II clearly affirmed the legitimacy of both the Church-to-Church and the one-by-one processes: "The work of preparing and reconciling those individuals who wish for full Catholic communion is of its nature distinct from ecumenical action. But there is no opposition between the two, since both proceed from the marvelous ways of God."[57]

In 1970, a Joint Working Group made up of representatives of the Catholic Church and the World Council of Churches published a discussion paper which attempted to deal with the difficult question of how Churches can receive members of other Churches into full communion without prejudicing the work of the ecumenical movement. The paper stated unambiguously: "While it is indeed aware of its pilgrim condition, a Church can be convinced that in it subsists the one Church founded by Christ, that also in it one can have access to all the means of salvation which the Lord offers, that its witness has always remained substantially faithful to the gospel. A Church can regard itself as bound in conscience to proclaim its witness to its own belief, which is distinct from that of the other Churches."[58]

The discussion paper also asserts the corresponding right of individuals to change their ecclesial allegiance in obedience to conscience. The receiving Church, it emphasizes, should be sure that people who make such a move are not doing so under pressure or to gain some material advantage; that they are acting with full knowledge and after consultation with pastors of both the Churches concerned; and that, if they are children, the views and rights of their parents are considered. Receiving Churches should avoid "vain glory," and Churches that lose a member should not become embittered.[59]

It is one thing to receive people who spontaneously

57. Vatican II, *Decree on Ecumenism*, n. 4.
58. *The Ecumenical Review*, XXIII: 1 (January, 1971), p. 14.
59. *Ibid.*, p. 18.

present themselves asking for full communion. But the parish also has to consider how far it wishes to go in actively urging individuals from other Christian bodies to join the Catholic Church. I am talking about legitimate witness to other Christians, of course, that rejects even the hint of unworthy proselytism. Legitimate witness is motivated by Christian love rather than institutional prestige; avoids moral or psychological pressure; does not exploit the need, weakness or lack of education of those to whom witness is offered; and refrains from unjust or uncharitable references to the beliefs or practices of other groups.[60] In the past, the Church has placed pastoral emphasis on the collective or the individual approach to unity, according to historical circumstances. Catholic-Orthodox relationships, for example, have been characterized by the collective approach.[61] I might suggest that active efforts to witness to other Christians one-by-one are more appropriate and desirable when directed toward members of those Churches that, from a Catholic theological viewpoint, contain only the barest minimum of ecclesial elements.

60. *Ibid.*, p. 16.
61. See the common declaration of Pope Paul VI and Patriarch Athenagoras I, on October 28, 1967. *AAS*, LIX: 16, p. 1054.

Challenge 5

EVANGELIZING THE UNCHURCHED

*To preach the gospel to the unchurched of
all categories and classes, inviting them
into full communion with the Church*

The unchurched are those whose ultimate values are not
reinforced through active participation in a Church.[62]
They are not necessarily irreligious in a broad sense. Most
of the unchurched people in this country have been exposed to religion at some point in their lives, and recent
studies indicate that all but a small minority believe in
God.[63] They remain religious *loners*, though. For one
reason or another—and the reasons can vary widely—they
do not see the importance of joining with other people in
a common search for God, for truth, for spiritual growth.

As Vatican II states, the "universal design of God for
the salvation of the human race is not carried out exclusively in the soul of an individual, with a kind of secrecy.
Nor is it achieved merely through those multiple endeavors, including religious ones, by which people search for
God. . . . All must be incorporated into Him by baptism,

62. "Unchurched" is a rather awkward term, but there seem to be few use-
ful alternatives.
63. See J. Russell Hale, *Who Are the Unchurched?* (Washington, D.C.:
Glenmary Research Center, 1977); David A. Roozen, *The Churched and the
Unchurched in America* (Washington, D.C.: Glenmary Research Center, 1978);
Edward A. Rauff, *Why People Join the Church* (Washington, D.C.: Glenmary
Research Center, 1979); *The Unchurched American* (Princeton, N.J.: The Gal-
lup Organization, 1978).

and into the Church which is His body.... [Therefore], a necessity lies upon the Church, and at the same time a sacred duty, to preach the gospel."[64]

The Church, then, must call people to that conversion of heart and fullness of faith that includes active participation in its own life.[65] Its ministry of evangelization intrudes on human consciousness, consoling and disturbing, shedding light on the mystery of existence, calling to repentance, affirming what is good and purifying what is evil. It communicates with power, in word and deed, the Life of the Trinity as revealed in Christ. Through evangelization, the members of the local Eucharistic community reach out to their brothers and sisters beyond the visible fellowship of organized religion, sharing in a bold but humble way the gifts they have received.

INDIRECT EVANGELIZATION

In *Evangelization in the Modern World*, Pope Paul VI describes indirect evangelization as *wordless witness*: "Above all the gospel must be proclaimed by witness. Take a Christian or a handfull of Christians who, in the midst of their own community, show their capacity for understanding and acceptance, their sharing of life and destiny with other people, their solidarity with the efforts of all for whatever is noble and good. Let us sup-

---

64. *Decree on the Church's Missionary Activity*, nn. 3 and 7.
65. As Paul VI and the Synod of 1974 state: "We wish to confirm once more that the task of evangelizing all people constitutes the essential mission of the Church." See Paul VI, *Apostolic Exhortation on Evangelization in the Modern World*, n. 14. See also David Bohr, *Evangelization in America* (New York: Paulist Press, 1977). These sources use "evangelization" in a broader sense than the evangelization of the unchurched, which is my topic here.

pose that, in addition, they radiate in an altogether simple and unaffected way their faith in values that go beyond current values, and their hope in something that is not seen and that one would not dare to imagine. Through this wordless witness these Christians stir up irresistible questions in the hearts of those who see how they live: Why are they like this? Why do they live in this way? What or who is it that inspires them? . . . Such a witness is already a silent proclamation of the good news and a very powerful and effective one."[66]

The parish contributes to this indispensable witness whenever it acts to promote the spiritual growth of its members or to become a warm and welcoming community of brothers and sisters in Christ. The other types of parish ministry also play an indirect part in evangelization. To the extent that the parish draws closer to other Christian groups, for example, it removes the scandal of disunity that can discourage people from joining the Church.[67] To the extent that it concerns itself with the poor and attempts to Christianize the social order, its members demonstrate how gospel values can be translated into everyday life.

I must mention here that non-parochial apostolates can play an important role in witnessing to the unchurched, too. A regional Catholic hospital, for example, can have a

66. Paul VI, *Evangelization*, n. 21.
67. Paul VI states: "The power of evangelization will find itself considerably diminished if those who proclaim the gospel are divided among themselves. . . . If the gospel that we proclaim is seen to be rent by doctrinal disputes, ideological polarizations or mutual condemnations among Christians, at the mercy of the latter's differing views on Christ and the Church and even because of their different concepts of society and human institutions, how can those to whom we address our preaching fail to be disturbed, disoriented, even scandalized?" *Evangelization*, n. 77.

significant impact, not because its specific purpose is evangelization, but because of the witness value of the health ministry that it is established to carry out. The same is true of a clinic, a house of prayer, or a social service agency that helps the poor. Ministries like these quietly manifest Catholic values, and parishioners should give them every encouragement and support.

DIRECT EVANGELIZATION

"The good news proclaimed by the witness of life sooner or later has to be proclaimed by the word of life."[68] The explicit act of evangelization is both a sign and an effect of commitment to the Lord. With the apostle Peter, Christians say, "We cannot but speak of what we have seen and heard" (Acts 4:20).

Because religion is a private matter in our culture, speaking about it to others is often difficult. Moreover, there is always the danger of personal rejection when people open themselves and reveal their most intimate values. With the help of grace, however, Catholics can break through the barriers of shyness and offer to others the reason for the hope that they have (1 Pet 3:15).

The invitation "to that fullness of faith and conversion which includes active participation in the Church" must be extended for the right reasons. Certainly church growth is a legitimate objective; increasing the number of members increases the congregation's ability to serve. But if this objective assumes *primary* importance in evangelization, the parish opens itself to the charge of compe-

---

68. Paul VI, *Evangelization*, n. 22.

titiveness and institutional self-seeking. The Catholic's overwhelming motivation must always be love for the people being evangelized, and gratitude to the Lord for His gifts and the privilege of sharing them with others. Like Pope John XXIII, the parish must somehow get across to the community at large that its main interest is the spiritual good of people, and that the well-being of the Church as an institution is fully subordinate to that value. The parish can demonstrate its sincerity by continuing to share its spiritual riches with the unchurched, and continuing to call them to the fullness of faith and conversion, even when there is little hope that they will ever actually join the congregation.

The motives of the unchurched are also important. Evangelizers must try to bring out in them the proper Christian motivation for conversion of heart and communion with the Church. A whole hierarchy of values usually enters into any important human decision. It is the evangelizer's responsibility to emphasize certain values over others and to clarify the relationships among them. Certainly the desire for religious security, spiritual comfort, self-fulfillment, esteem, prestige, emotional experience, and a sense of belonging could all consciously or unconsciously affect a person's decision to join the Church. But evangelization must make clear that all these things are subordinate to the love of God and neighbor, and to the desire to participate in a Eucharistic community that offers a share in the divine life both here and hereafter.

Further, there can be no call to Christian conversion without a simultaneous call to the cross. New members can expect to find what they seek—contact with the Lord, spiritual comfort, religious security—in the Catholic parish.

But because of sin, and because the congregation is still part of a Pilgrim People, they will not find these things unmixed with pain and frustration. The experience of the cross within the Eucharistic community completes the work the evangelizer begins: purifying Christian motivation, promoting self-transcendence, and setting values in their right relationships to one another. Evangelization that failed to stress this reality would be unfaithful to the gospel.[69]

An attitude of deep respect for others should mark the Catholic who wishes to share the Faith. There is no room for pride, as though God's life were not a free gift and the evangelizer not a sinner. We cannot read the secrets of hearts; for all we know, the unchurched person we approach may have lived more faithful to grace than we. Pride may provoke a backlash, too—especially in mission areas where conservative evangelicals predominate and the unchurched are bombarded on all sides with invitations "to accept the Lord Jesus and be saved." People tend to react against certain evangelists who speak before listening, and who expect everyone to respond enthusiastically to a pre-formulated appeal. *True evangelizers will first listen, to discern how God is working in the unchurched person. Then when they do speak, their words will reflect a spirit of praise for the Lord's favors and an accurate appreciation of the other's spiritual state.*

What can the parish do to carry out a program of evangelization? First of all, it can *pray*. The congregation should pray frequently that God will grant unbelievers the

69. William Ashdown, *Motivation and Response in Religion* (Cincinnati: Glenmary Department of Research, 1962), pp. 139 ff.

precious gift of faith, that He will help those with an unformed faith to understand the importance of joining the ecclesial community, and that He will inspire Catholics to care enough to reach out.

Second, the parish can *offer its members encouragement and support* in ministering as individual Christians to their unchurched relatives, friends, neighbors and business associates. Collective encouragement can help potential evangelizers overcome their reluctance to talk openly about religion. Group instruction and discussion can provide perspective, giving evangelizers insights into their own motivation and the motivation they should foster in the unchurched. And the strength they receive from the supporting community can stimulate them to approach their task with that humble boldness mentioned above.

Third, the parish can operate *programs* whose specific goal is evangelization of the unchurched. A half-dozen people can meet to pray and exchange experiences, for example, as they systematically make contact with unbelievers, perhaps through the informal network of relationships that small town society affords. (Sometimes groups like these get early assistance from religious or lay volunteers who come into the mission area especially to render that service.) Prayer groups or inquiry classes can be organized to accommodate those who need a halfway house on the road to the Church, those who have a strong interest in Catholicism but are not yet ready for membership. Finally, the parish can carry out a newspaper, radio or television ministry aimed not just at potential Catholics but at all the county's residents.

In all this an attempt must be made to reach the unchurched of all social strata, including the lowest. Experience has shown that more time and effort is needed to reach members of the lower class than members of the other groups, simply because relationships within that class are more casual and personal. In a previous section I spoke about the need for a special effort to prepare the Catholic community to welcome such people. A similar effort will be required to evangelize them in the first place.

Also, there must be a "collaboration . . . with the Christian brethren with whom we are not yet united in perfect unity, taking as a basis the foundation of Baptism and the patrimony of faith which is common to us. By doing this we can already give a greater common witness to Christ before the world in the very work of evangelization."[70] This collaboration does not mean that the differences among the various denominations should be blurred, of course. If we share many elements with other Churches, we also have certain differences. The Catholic parish has the responsibility to offer the unchurched of the community a true religious option. The challenge is to present our common Christian heritage and, at the same time, without competitiveness or falsification, to express the fullness of our Catholic vision in faithfulness to the Lord.

---

70. Paul VI, *Evangelization*, n. 77.

Challenge 6

SOCIAL ACTION

To minister to people in need, and to help create a more just and beneficial social order

The picture of the Last Judgment painted in Matthew's Gospel leaves no doubt that practical concern for the needs of others is a strict requirement for entrance into the kingdom of heaven. We will be judged precisely on our ability to see the Lord in our neighbor: "As long as you did it for one of these, the least of my brethren, you did it for me" (Mt 25:40). There are as many ways to help others in rural counties as there are urgent and immediate needs. The Christian can offer food and clothing to those who cannot help themselves; can comfort the bereaved; encourage the alcoholic; shelter the burned-out family; offer companionship to the sick and elderly; contribute financially to the relief of those in emergency situations; visit prisoners; counsel those undergoing personal crises; aid transients. Like the Good Samaritan, we must respond with love to the people with whom we associate day by day (Lk 10:30-37).

But love of neighbor requires even more of us than satisfying individual needs. We must also work toward creating a social environment where people are free to grow in the Life of the Trinity given to us through Christ. This means trying to shape social systems. The Christian should bring moral judgment to bear on the economic, political, educational, recreational and familial systems that provide the context for ordinary life, and should try to make them more just. As Vatican II states: "When people develop the earth by the work of their hands or with the aid of technology, in order that it might bear fruit and become a dwelling worthy of the whole human family and when they consciously take part in the life of social groups, they carry out the design of God manifested at the beginning of time, that they should subdue the earth, perfect creation and develop themselves. At the same time they obey the commandment of Christ that they place themselves at the service of [others]."[71]

The 1971 Synod of Bishops underlined the importance of the justice dimension of social ministry: "Action on behalf of justice and participation in the transformation of the world fully appear to us as a constitutive dimension of the preaching of the gospel...."[72] To transform the world is to make social systems contribute to the common good, rather than favoring some people or classes at the expense of others. Concern for the dignity of all impels the Church to take the part of the poor and the powerless in the search for a more equitable society.[73]

The effort to renew social systems can take many forms. In the political sphere, for example, Christians should help guarantee the kind of government that is open to widespread citizen participation and deeply committed to the common good. In the economic sphere, they might place special emphasis on programs that aid dependent

71. Vatican II, *Pastoral Constitution on the Church in the Modern World*, n. 57. See also Vatican II, n. 36.
72. 1971 Synod of Bishops, *Justice in the World*, Introduction.
73. *Ibid.*, Chapter I.

children and other helpless people. Depending on local circumstances, a massive effort might be needed to improve the educational system, to provide transportation, to improve health care, to develop family services, to increase general recreational opportunities, or to generate interest in the advancement of culture and the arts. Finally, there is a range of justice issues relating to racial prejudice, the right to life, or people's right to their good name, so often violated in rural communities by vicious gossip.

Ministry to social systems and ministry to our neighbor's immediate needs are complementary expressions of Christian love. Both are necessary. We must not become so engrossed in solving the economic and social problems of the aging in America that we have no time for the little old lady next door.[74] On the other hand, the love that prompts us to respond to people's immediate and personal needs should lead naturally to a desire to change the conditions that create those needs in the first place. Our approach to social action should recognize that human beings exist simultaneously as individuals and as members of society.

INDIRECT SOCIAL ACTION

The renewal of the temporal order must spring from the seedbed of personal relationships with Christ.[75] The love of God is the only motive that can sustain the effort to

---

74. See Peter Berger, *The Noise of Solemn Assemblies* (New York: Doubleday, 1961), p. 141.

75. See Pope Paul VI, *Apostolic Exhortation on Evangelization in the Modern World*, n. 20.

serve our neighbor in the long run, especially in the face of frustration, disappointment and lack of response. Moreover, an orientation to spiritual realities is essential to prevent Christian service from degenerating into the mere promotion of consumerism, where we help people to improve their material condition with no thought of higher values.[76] The parish, therefore, contributes in some way to social action whenever it nurtures its members' spiritual life and calls all people to conversion of heart. It is fostering the vision that gives strength and direction to service of others.

DIRECT SOCIAL ACTION

As a small-scale organization with a primary focus on the individual, the parish is in an excellent position to minister in a neighborly way to people in need. This *ministry to immediate needs* can consist of congregational prayer for particular individuals and concerns. The parish can also try to sensitize its members to the hurts and wants of their neighbors in the community. It can teach the correct Christian motivation for service. It can encourage parishioners to exercise charity, and to participate in the charitable work of civic and religious organizations. It can get involved as a parish with these same organizations—civic groups, public or private agencies, Catholic or ecumenical ministries—and give them its moral and financial support. Finally, it can operate certain service ministries of its

76. See Vatican II, *Pastoral Constitution on the Church in the Modern World*, n. 43.

own.[77] This is most appropriate when there is little likelihood that urgent needs will be met in any other way.

Christians are only stewards of the material goods God has provided; they must never offer help in a spirit of condescension. Neither should they permit their honest service to foster unhealthy dependencies in those who receive it, dependencies that threaten human dignity or self-determination. Most importantly, they must not allow the ministry to immediate needs to become a palliative that weakens or dissipates their commitment to the urgent struggle for justice.

Generally speaking, *ministry to social systems* is more complicated than ministry to immediate needs, because the sources of systemic influence often lie outside the community.[78] A multi-national corporation, for example, may own the local factory. The county government, the social service agencies and the schools may all be highly dependent on state and federal support. Even recreation is shaped in part by music, films and television programs produced at the national level. Nevertheless, parishioners can have an impact on "the way things are," especially if they are willing to join with other people in large-scale efforts aimed at social renewal.[79]

77. Vatican II states: "When circumstances of time and place produce the need, [the Church] can and indeed should initiate activities on behalf of all men, especially those designed for the needy, such as the works of mercy and similar undertakings." *Pastoral Constitution on the Church in the Modern World*, n. 42.

78. See Arthur J. Vidich and Joseph Bensman, *Small Town in Mass Society: Class, Power and Religion in a Rural Community* (Princeton University Press, 1968), and Roland L. Warren, *The Community in America* (Chicago: Rand McNally, 1963).

79. Some national organizations that provide rural resource materials for ministry to social systems are: the National Catholic Rural Life Conference, 4625. N.W. Beaver Drive, Des Moines, Iowa 50322; the Parish Outreach Pro-

The first thing the parish can do is pray for the community and its political, economic and educational leaders. Secondly, it can organize programs, not necessarily designed for Catholics alone, that explain the Church's social teaching. Such programs might stress the rights and duties of people in society, the importance of social action, and the concept of the common good.[80]

Thirdly, the parish can support its members as they act in their own names as baptized Christians to renew the social order. On one level, such support might involve setting up a group that helps people in a given occupation explore ways in which they can exert Christian influence through that occupation. What could farmers do *as farmers*, for example? On another level, it might take the form of general encouragement to participate in secular, Catholic or ecumenical organizations that are working on a particular justice issue or attempting to affect some social system.[81] Imagination will suggest a variety of possibilities.

People's attitudes toward social questions are often conditioned by their political philosophies. As a result, Catholics will often disagree among themselves on the concrete application of a principle, or the means to be

gram of the National Conference of Catholic Charities, 1346 Connecticut Avenue, N.W., Washington, D.C. 20036; and the Department of Domestic Social Development of the United States Catholic Conference, 1312 Massachusetts Avenue, N.W., Washington, D.C. 20005.

80. Chapter III of the 1971 Synod of Bishops speaks about the Church's obligation to educate for justice.

81. Community organizing is one of the most widely used approaches to ministry to social systems. For a detailed discussion, see Harry Fagan, *Empowerment: Skills for Parish Social Action* (New York: Paulist Press, 1979), and Irwin T. Sanders, *Making Good Communities Better* (Lexington: University of Kentucky Press, 1953).

followed in achieving a desired goal. This disagreement is perfectly legitimate and, where competent authority has not taken an official stand, individuals should avoid stifling debate by giving the impression that they speak in the name of the Church. As Vatican II states, "No one is allowed . . . to appropriate the Church's authority exclusively for his own opinion."[82] This caution applies with special force to pastors and other vocational church workers, because listeners tend to invest their words with ecclesial weight unless they make clear that they are speaking as individual Christians voicing their individual points of view.

According to Vatican II, "Christ . . . gave His Church no proper mission in the political, economic or social order. The purpose which He set before her is a religious one. But out of this religious mission itself comes a function, a light and an energy which can serve to structure and consolidate the human community according to the divine law."[83] It follows that the parish can best serve the social order by calling Catholics and others to fulfill their own proper responsibilities in the world.

There are circumstances, however, in which providing such general guidance is not enough. The parish, acting in the light of the Church's clear teaching, may have to speak out on local issues from time to time. It may have to lend its name or its moral or financial support to organizations promoting renewal. If no other way lies open, it may even have to take direct action using its own members and resources.[84] These demonstrations of loyalty to

82. Vatican II, *Pastoral Constitution on the Church in the Modern World*, n. 43.
83. *Ibid.*, n. 42.
84. *Ibid.*

Christian principles have the potential to disturb congregational tranquility,[85] or cause a loss of prestige or
influence in the community. Should that happen, the parish must remember, without indulging in self-righteous-
ness, that it is sometimes called to share in the passion
and death of the Lord.

Challenge 7

CATHOLICITY

*To participate in the apostolate of the
Church at the world, national, diocesan
and other levels*

The parish must show concern for dimensions of the apostolate that are beyond its own immediate local responsibility. It must participate generously in the universal
work of the Church, remembering the words of the Lord,
"Give, and it shall be given to you; good measure, pres-
sed down, shaken together, running over . . ." (Lk 6:38).
In this way it expresses its catholicity, shows gratitude for
what it has received, and deepens its spirit of dedication.

In the first place, the parish must cooperate in the *missionary activity* of the Church, whereby "heralds of the
gospel [are sent] until such time as infant churches are

---

85. In many mission counties, for example, factory managers and workers
are members of the same parish.

fully established. . . ."[86] The parish is to pray for the missions; familiarize its members with the missionary situation; foster priestly, religious and lay missionary vocations; offer financial assistance; and provide moral support.

It should take part, too, in the *general ministry* of the wider Church, whether that ministry is carried out in mission areas or elsewhere. This again involves prayer, education, the fostering of vocations, financial assistance, and moral support. Such aid could be directed at any or all of the tasks the Church addresses: the spiritual development of Catholics, ecumenism, evangelization, social action.

While demonstrating its concern for the Church at the international, national and diocesan levels, the parish should not miss opportunities for cooperation closer to home. Sometimes regional or interparochial organizations share its territory, carrying out ministries of their own.[87] Pastors and parishioners must resist the temptation to compete against these apostolates, and must instead offer every help they can. All, they must remind themselves, are part of one body in Christ.

---

86. Vatican II, *Dogmatic Constitution on the Church*, n. 17. See also Vatican II, *Decree on the Church's Missionary Activity*, n. 6.

87. For a discussion of these non-parochial ministries, see David Byers, *New Directions for the Rural Church* (New York: Paulist Press, 1978).

III

Stages of
Parish Development

As it responds to the seven challenges outlined in the last chapter, a rural parish will become a community. If it responds to them well, it will become a vital community—one with a many-faceted ministry where people of various levels of commitment find support for their ordinary, everyday Christian witness and life.

Clearly, however, the parish will not reach this level all at once. "For the Church, although of itself including the totality or fullness of the means of salvation, does not and cannot always and instantly bring them all into action. Rather, she experiences beginnings and degrees in that action by which she strives to make God's plan a reality."[1] The parish develops. Like a human being, it passes through various stages from birth to adulthood, and each stage is characterized by a different set of priorities, goals and constraints. A parish is born when the Catholics living in a certain area first assemble around the Lord's

---

1. Vatican II, *Decree on the Church's Missionary Activity*, n. 6.

table for regular Sunday liturgy. Soon, usually with help from the outside, the Eucharistic community begins to generate ongoing, organized ministries of nurture and outreach. The years pass and, through advances and setbacks, it matures into a stable congregation with its own local resources and local roots.

An awareness of these stages can be helpful. Parishes often experience debilitating stress and anxiety because what is expected of them (and what they expect of themselves) is entirely unrelated to where they are on the continuum of development. This anxiety is both unfortunate and unnecessary. A baby cannot have the intellectual or emotional sophistication of a child, a teenager or an adult. Neither can a small parish have all the programs and activities of one that is more advanced. An approach which relates expectations to development level is a better starting point for enthusiasm and creativity.

I intend to describe here three stages the rural parish passes through on its way to adulthood: initial gathering, intensification and localization.[2] My purpose is to offer perspective on parish life and growth. At each stage the parish needs to address all seven challenges, but it will address them in different ways. One aspect of a given challenge will receive emphasis in one stage, for example, and a second aspect in another. In discussing the challenges, I presented a snapshot of an ideal. Here I hope to produce a motion picture of a process: how a parish, step by step, translates the ideal into reality.

---

2. Although based on field observation, the description of the three stages is provisional and subject to further refinement.

Stage 1

INITIAL GATHERING

In the beginning, Catholics in a mission county may meet for an occasional Mass celebrated by a visiting priest. Or there may be a prayer group with a stable membership and schedule, or even a catechumenate for potential converts. A parish is actually established, however, only when a pastor (or his representative) is formally sent by the Church to organize the faithful into a Eucharistic community where the Word is regularly preached and the Sacraments are regularly celebrated. From that time on, the Catholics in that place constitute a new entity in the Church, and their group life has a special ecclesial status.[3]

The first priority in this stage is *to gather the Catholics together.* This involves contacting the practicing and non-practicing and inviting them to participate in the new parish; organizing the celebration of the Eucharist and other Sacraments; making provision, at least in an elementary way, for religious instruction; and helping the people get acquainted with one another.

There will often be a few Catholics, natives or newcomers, whose commitment to the Lord and to the Church is deep and strong, and who have expressed that commitment over the years by traveling many miles to participate in a Eucharistic community. These people need support in continuing their spiritual development. Others may need basic evangelization, not just to encourage their

---

3. See Canons 216 and 451 ff.

attendance at Mass, but also to bring about a real conversion to the Lord.

In addition, the parishioners as a group must come to
understand how the Church expresses its presence in the
very first stages of missionary activity. Those who have
moved in from heavily Catholic places, for example, must
learn to accept mission constraints. They cannot expect
the full range of ministries (such as Catholic schools) in
this setting. At the same time, there is need to broaden
people's horizons. The parish cannot remain content with
nurturing its own members; in mission areas especially,
outreach is of very great significance.

The second priority is to develop that outreach by *open-
ing up opportunities for the parish to minister to the
community at large.* Mission areas are not generally
hostile to the Catholic Church, but a new congregation
presents local people with an unfamiliar phenomenon. In
order to accustom the community to Catholic ministry,
the parish will welcome promising opportunities for service, whether this service is directed at the most important needs or not. For example, it will promote ecumenical
relationships with the groups that express an interest in
it, even if they do not represent the largest religious bodies
in the county. It will approach those unchurched people
who give most sign of being ready for evangelization. And
it will accept invitations to cooperate with appropriate
civic and social organizations whose work is useful though
perhaps not urgent.

In the beginning, lay participation in all these ministries
will inevitably be small; there will only be a handful of
Catholics with enough commitment to play an active part.
Consequently, the pastor and other vocational church

workers will have to carry much of the burden, and they will find themselves reaching out to the community in ways that go beyond the expectations and the theological vision of many parishioners. They must be careful to do so, however, precisely as members of the Catholic community, not apart from it.[4] That is, they must involve the laity as much as possible, given the realities of the missionary situation. And they must try to hasten the day when the congregation assumes its proper role in carrying out all the tasks which the Church has committed to the local parish.

Indicators that a rural mission parish has reached the conclusion of its first stage of development include the following:

1. The basic Sacramental ministries are organized and ongoing, and regular provision is made for the instruction of adults and children, even if this instruction is quite limited in scope.

2. For at least a few Catholics, religion is more than just external practices; it involves personal commitment to the Lord.

3. There is some outreach in terms of ecumenism, evangelization, social action and concern for the wider Church, though these efforts may be minimal and not yet formally organized.

4. A climate of good will has been created in the community, at least to the extent that the parish is no longer seen as a new or strange phenomenon and its ministry is welcome.

---

4. For this reason, outside church workers should not be so numerous as to overwhelm the local congregation.

5. The parishioners know one another, some of them are actively involved in ministries of nurture or outreach, and they contribute to parish support, whether or not the church is financially independent.

Stage 2
INTENSIFICATION

The first priority in the intensification stage is *to deepen the spiritual life of Catholics*. On the most basic level, the leadership must work to improve the quality of public prayer and the effectiveness of instructional programs for adults and children. It is even more important, however, to arrange for parishioners to engage in occasional activities that are specifically designed to bring their faith alive: missions, days of recollection, retreats, Cursillos, Search programs, Marriage Encounters and the like. Peak experiences of this sort can be a real leap forward, providing spiritual momentum and stimulating a conversion of heart. Individuals can sustain this momentum through renewed participation in the regular Eucharistic celebration and other parish activities including, where feasible, prayer groups set up especially for their mutual support.

The second priority is *to begin the formal organization of ministries of outreach to the community at large*. As far as ecumenism is concerned, this means establishing contact with several religious bodies including, if possible, at least one denomination that is strongly represented in the area.[5] In evangelization, it means initi-

5. What I mean by "establishing contact" is explained in Chapter II under Challenge 4.

ating some program—perhaps a very modest one—aimed at touching the unchurched.[6] In the social apostolate, it means organizing an effort to address immediate needs, especially those of the poor.[7] (Through such a ministry, Christians will begin to see Christ in others and grow sensitive to the need for engaging in the more difficult ministry to social systems.)[8] Finally, it means giving some formal expression to the parish's catholicity, not only by contributing financially to the work of the wider Church, but also by becoming informed on issues and praying for specific intentions.[9]

As a mission community not yet possessing all the resources needed for its life and witness, the parish can rightly call on the Church at large for help.[10] Outside help is especially useful in the second stage of development, both in the form of vocational church workers—Brothers, Sisters, lay volunteers—and the funding that makes their presence possible. These missioners can take

---

6. See Chapter II, Challenge 5.

7. See Chapter II, Challenge 6.

8. It is even possible that some ministry to social systems will be organized at this stage.

9. See Chapter II, Challenge 7.

10. Vatican II states: "As members of the living Christ, incorporated into Him and made like unto Him through baptism and through confirmation and the Eucharist, all the faithful are duty-bound to cooperate in the expansion and spreading out of His Body, to bring it to fullness as soon as may be." And again: "All bishops, as members of the body of bishops succeeding to the College of Apostles, are consecreated not just for some one diocese, but for the salvation of the entire world. The mandate of Christ to preach the Gospel to every creature (Mk 16:15) primarily and immediately concerns them, with Peter and under Peter. Whence there arises that communion and cooperation of Churches which is so necessary today for carrying on the work of evangelization. In virtue of this communion, the individual Churches bear the burden of care for them all, and make their necessities known to one another...." *Decree on the Church's Missionary Activity*, nn. 36 and 38.

the lead in launching ongoing programs that range in their focus from worship, religious instruction and spiritual counseling to ecumenism, evangelization and social action. Without such aid, it is unlikely that the average parish will be able to develop truly effective ministries within a reasonable length of time. Moreover, the missioners can share their vision and expertise with the laity. If they do so in the proper spirit, always encouraging maximum local ownership of the work, they will gradually and gently equip the parishioners for the tasks and responsibilities that are properly theirs.

In this connection, it is essential that outside church workers do not initiate permanent, specialized ministries that the parish will be unable to carry on after it has reached adulthood. The goal of the parish is to create a vital Eucharistic community that reaches out to the community at large in a general and rather simple way; it can never meet all the area's needs. Specialized ministries that address these urgent needs must be encouraged, of course, and the parish should cooperate with them in every way. But they are best established outside the parochial framework, with independent funding. Parish programs should be planned in such a way that, in the post-missionary stage, they can be continued on a regular basis by the pastor and laity and such vocational church workers as the financial resources of a small congregation could conceivably sustain.

Indicators that a rural mission parish has reached the conclusion of its second stage of development include the following:

1. The basic Sacramental and educational ministries are well organized, and parishioners have at least

occasional opportunities to participate in special programs of spiritual intensification.

2. Enough Catholics have internalized their religion and broadened their vision of the Church's mission that there is reasonable hope that a parish council can be vital and effective.

3. Ministries of ecumenism, evangelization of the un-churched, social action and concern for the wider Church are organized and ongoing.

4. Out of a sense of Christian responsibility, at least a few parishioners are actively involved, formally or informally, in each parish ministry of nurture and outreach, and individuals are beginning to exercise leadership in some of them.

Stage 3

LOCALIZATION

The first priority in this stage is *to expand the organized ministries of outreach, and to make sure that they touch all significant social classes and ethnic/racial groups in the community*. The leadership should begin to instruct parishioners about other denominations in the area and, ideally, should open up formal ecumenical dialogue with at least one non-Catholic congregation. By this time, there should be contact with Churches whose membership reflects each major social grouping, including the lowest class.[11] Programs for evangelizing the unchurched of all social strata must be established, with special emphasis

11. See Chapter II, Challenge 4.

on the poor.[12] And social action must now include not only ministry to immediate needs, but ministry to social systems as well.[13]

The second priority is *to prepare the congregation psychologically and physically for life as an adult parish.* The pastor and his council should work to provide the buildings and other facilities needed for ongoing ministry, if they are not already in place.[14] More importantly, they must shape the Catholic community so that it warmly welcomes outsiders of all social classes and racial/ethnic groups. Achieving this difficult objective requires careful planning; the parish may wish to employ one or more of the approaches suggested in the discussion of community in Chapter 2.[15]

As the parish nears the end of the missionary period, its lay members will begin to assume greater responsibility for ministries of nurture and outreach, a task for which the pastor and other staff members have helped them prepare. The parish council, under the overall leadership of the pastor, should by now be playing a prominent and significant role in the life of the congregation. At the same time, the parish will work toward becoming a self-supporting entity, capable of providing from its own resources the funds needed for its staff and for other elements of its ministry. Once it attains financial viability, it should contribute even more generously to missionary activity in other areas.

---

12. See Chapter II, Challenge 5.
13. See Chapter II, Challenge 6.
14. A mission parish often receives outside assistance in making such one-time capital outlays.
15. See Chapter II, Challenge 1.

The following are indicators that a parish has passed beyond the third and final stage of missionary development:

1. The Catholic community is stable, self-supporting, and has enough members to provide diversification in ministry; local Catholics include people from all major social and racial-ethnic groups.

2. The parish has the full range of organized ministries of nurture and outreach that is suitable for its size and the area's needs.

3. The parish exhibits spiritual vitality, both in its group life and in the lives of many of its members.

4. Under the overall leadership of the pastor, the laity are involved actively and responsibly in parish ministries of nurture and outreach at every level.

When these conditions have been met, a local Catholic community has been truly planted in a given locality, and its presence, alongside other important ministries, constitutes a substantial and ongoing contribution to the Church's saving work.

PLANNING

As the parish passes through the various stages of development, hard decisions have to be made about its ministry and life. These decisions require a great deal of thought and reflection. People are coming to realize that reflection is itself an important dimension of parish ministry, requiring both time and energy. When the process of thinking about the parish and its growth is carried out in a formal, systematic and regular way, the result is planning.

For all its bureaucratic associations, planning can be one way of attempting to be faithful to the Spirit. If based on purely secular values, of course, planning can do more harm than good. On the other hand, if it is prayerful—if it reflects the Church's mystery and relies heavily on grace—it focuses human skills on accomplishing what is basically a spiritual work.[16]

Planning involves reflection by the parish leadership on the theology of the Church's task, on the needs and circumstances of a particular time and place, on the resources of the congregation, and on the priorities (for both nurture and outreach) within a given stage of development. A positive outlook is important. Planning should begin with a review of accomplishments, not a list of failures. And it should end with a sense of commitment, so that the parish, while fully conscious of current limitations, will be ready to extend itself in the Lord's work.[17]

Prayerful planning, based on an accurate assessment of the parish's development, helps create an atmosphere of serenity conducive to growth. At the same time, the honest recognition of constraints fosters humility and encourages dependence on God's power. We know that the cross is always present; setbacks and disappointments will arise both within the congregation and outside it. Yet if the rural mission parish has a reflective vision of where the Lord is leading, it can adopt a resurrection perspective and face its challenges with confidence and courage.

---

16. For a detailed discussion of this point, see Bernard Quinn, *Theological Reflections on the Planning Process* (Washington, D.C.: Glenmary Research Center, 1972).

17. The Glenmary Research Center has developed a planning process for small rural parishes called *Reflective Ministry*.

Appendix A

How to Determine Parish Priorities

A small rural parish that wishes to determine its priorities according to the guidelines described in this book can do so by following a relatively simple procedure. Three steps are involved: (1) preparing a progress report for the parish; (2) determining the present stage of parish development; and (3) in light of 1 and 2, setting priorities appropriate for this parish at this stage of development. Suggestions for implementing the three steps are given below. The suggestions are followed by a sample Priority Statement that will give the reader a concrete model to work from.

I

How to Draft a Priority Statement

Step 1

PREPARING A PROGRESS REPORT

INTRODUCTION. Give the name of the parish, the town in which the principal church is located, the name and location of mission churches. If it is a territorial parish, list the counties (or part counties) within the parish boundaries, the approximate area the parish covers in square miles and the total population. Indicate the number of Catholics (including those at least occasional in religious practice), the number of other Christians and the number of the unchurched in the area; state the percentage that each group represents of the total population.[1] State the area's principal social characteristics: population gain or loss, racial/ethnic composition, principal sources of jobs, and prevalence of poverty.[2] If this report does not cover the entire parish area, adjust the statistics to reflect the portion it does cover.

PARISH PROGRAMS. Under each of the following categories, describe the programs of ministry that the parish is currently engaged in: (1) Catholic nurture; (2) seeking Christian unity; (3) evangelizing the unchurched; (4) social action; (5) catholicity (concern for the wider Church).

First, write down all the parish *activities* you can think of on five sheets of paper, one for each of the categories mentioned above. The Checklist of Activities (see below), parish bulletins, annual reports and financial records will be useful in compiling this inventory. Although much of the Church's ministry is exercised by individual Christians acting in virtue of their baptismal commitment and mandate, only those activities that are somehow "of" the parish—carried out by the parish as an organization—should be included. In practice, most activities of the pastor and other staff will be considered to be "of" the parish, as will those which parishioners perform as members of parish organizations or as participants in parish life. Group activities specifically designed to encourage parishioners in their own ministries as individual Christians should be listed.

Once the inventory is complete, group the various activities into programs. Programs are clusters of activities organized and operated together. Since parishes vary in the organization of their ministries, no two parishes will have exactly the same program list, even when their activities are similar.

---

1. County statistics on other Christians are available from *Churches and Church Membership in the United States* (Washington, D.C.: Glenmary Research Center).

2. See U.S. Census, *County and City Data Book*, available in most local libraries.

A CHECKLIST OF PARISH ACTIVITIES

1. NURTURE OF CATHOLICS

Worship: Sunday worship and homily? other regular worship in church? at home? provision for the Sacrament of Reconciliation? prayer groups? seasonal devotions? special celebration of feasts?

Christian Education: children? adults? families?

Life Events: sacramental ministries, religious counseling, pastoral visitation, instructions, other ministries relating to life events: birth, vocational choice, marriage, death, poverty, illness, special problems, interpersonal crises, and the like?

Intensification: occasional ministries to deepen religious experience: parish missions? parish days of recollection? encouraging parishioners to participate in retreats, Cursillos, Search Programs, Marriage Encounters and the like?

Categories of Persons: ministries for single, married, separated, widowed persons? families? children and teens? young adults? men? women? older persons? residents of military barracks? boarders in schools or colleges? hospital residents? prisoners? people in rest homes, orphanages, seasonal youth camps? migrant workers? seasonal leisure residents? tourists/vacationers?

Parish Organizations: prayer groups? committees? societies? other?

Socials: recreational events that promote parish community?

Other ministries of Catholic nurture?

2. SEEKING CHRISTIAN UNITY

Ministries of Friendliness? ministerial associations? general?

Congregational Contact: with denominations having few members in the area? with predominant denominations? with churches of the poor?

Prayer for Unity: in conjunction with other Christians? separately?

Instruction about other Churches?

Ecumenical Dialogue: formal dialogue with small denominations? with predominant denominations?

Reconciling individual Christians to the Church?

Supporting the informal ecumenical ministry of parishioners: prayer? instruction? developing confidence and skills?

Other ministries for promoting Christian unity?

3. EVANGELIZING THE UNCHURCHED

Prayer for the conversion of the unchurched?

Supporting the informal ministry of parishioners to the unchurched: prayer? instruction? developing confidence and skills?

Organized ministry: visitation? contact through informal networks?

Educational/Prayer Experiences for the unchurched: prayer groups? inquiry classes? Bible schools? preparation for profession of faith (catechumenate)? other?

Categories of Persons: social/ethnic groups? the poor? other social classes? single persons? married? separated? widowed? families? children and teens? young adults? men? women? older persons? residents of military barracks? boarders in schools or colleges? hospital residents? prisoners? people in rest homes, orphanages, seasonal youth camps? migrant workers? seasonal leisure residents? tourists/vacationers? rural/town residents?

Media ministry: radio? newspaper? television?

Other ministries for evangelizing the unchurched?

4. SOCIAL ACTION

MINISTRY TO IMMEDIATE NEEDS

Categories of Need: food, clothing, shelter, funds, jobs, transportation, job training, education, medical care, legal services, recreational opportunities, companionship, secular counseling?

Prayer for persons in need?

Supporting the ministry of parishioners in serving persons in immediate need: prayer? sensitizing to needs? instruction? developing confidence and skills?

Parish Sponsorship/Support of Organizations established to meet individual needs: public agencies? private? ecumenical? Catholic non-parochial?

Organized parish ministries for meeting immediate needs?

MINISTRY TO SOCIAL SYSTEMS

Categories of Systems: economic, political, educational, recreational, familial?

Issues: community development, industrial relations, agriculture, political empowerment, health services, educational opportunities, housing, welfare, transportation, conservation, environment, right to life, culture and the arts, freedom from slander, freedom from discrimination because of race, sex, class or creed?

Prayer for the restoration of the temporal order in Christ?

Education about Catholic social principles: radio? newspaper? television? lectures? instructions? symbolic actions?

Supporting the Ministry of Parishioners as they act in their own names as baptized Christians to renew the social order: support groups? prayer? instruction? developing insight, confidence, skills?

Ministries in the Name of the Parish: sponsorship or support of organizations working for social renewal? statements applying Catholic social principles to specific issues?

Other ministries to social systems?

5. CATHOLICITY (CONCERN FOR THE WIDER CHURCH)

   Cooperating in Missionary Activity: prayer? sensitizing people to mission needs? fostering vocations? financial assistance? moral support?

   Cooperating in the General Ministry of the Church: international? diocesan? regional? prayer? sensitizing to needs? fostering vocations? financial assistance? moral support? preparing parishioners to cooperate with and work in apostolates beyond the parish?

When you have compiled your list of parish programs, write a brief description of each program. The description should include (where appropriate): (1) the program's present activities and plans for the immediate future; (2) whom the program serves; (3) who participates actively in ministry, as leaders or otherwise; (4) how the program is organized, including the lines of accountability; (5) the sources of current funding; (6) whether the program is designed to continue beyond the missionary stage, and if so, how it will probably be funded.

THE PARISH AS A COMMUNITY. By answering the following questions about its group life, the parish will obtain a sense of how far it has developed as a community.

1. HISTORY: Date established? Principal events?

2. SIZE: Number of Catholics regular in religious practice? occasional in practice? total? Catholic percent of the population?

3. SPIRTUALITY: How many Catholics have a strong Catholic identity, have internalized their religion, and have a vision of ministry that goes beyond congregational nurture? To what extent does prayer enter into planning, and into the programs and activities of the parish?

4. LOCAL ROOTS: Based on the previous history of growth or decline, what can be said about the future stability of the Catholic

congregation? Does the parish contain members of the significant social groups found in the community as a whole?[3]

5. STAFF: Besides the pastor, are there other vocational church workers or volunteers? What staff is anticipated when the parish is no longer in the missionary stage and must depend on its own financial resources?

6. PARTICIPATION: What percent of the Catholics participate in formal parish programs of nurture and outreach, as active ministers and as leaders? What percent of the Catholics participate informally in ministry to one another? What percent participate informally as individual Christians in ministries of outreach?

7. COMMUNITY OPENNESS: What plans does the parish have for structuring the Catholic community to embrace persons of diverse ethnic/racial groups and all social classes, including the poor?

8. FINANCES: To what extent is the parish presently self-supporting? What is the source of outside funds, if any? What is the stability of present funding (is it unduly dependent on a few)? To what extent can present funding be reasonably increased?

9. FACILITIES: What facilities does the parish have available? Are they rented or owned by the Church? What is needed to accommodate the programs of an adult congregation?

10. PLANNING: Is there a process for overall planning? Is there an active and effective parish council? Is there good communication within the parish?

---

3. A good way to identify the significant social groups is to obtain statistics from the U.S. Census on the county's racial/ethnic make-up, income categories, age structure, educational profile and the ratio of newcomers to long-term residents.

Step 2

DETERMINING THE PRESENT STAGE
OF PARISH DEVELOPMENT

Consult Chapter III for the list of indicators for each stage of parish development. Locate your parish in Stage 1, 2 or 3. If the parish fulfills some requirements for the completion of a given stage but not all of them, it has not passed beyond that stage. For example, a parish with highly developed ministries of nurture but no outreach whatsoever would still be in Stage 1.

Write a few paragraphs defending your judgment. If you have placed the parish in Stage 2, for example, explain how it has passed stage 1 but has not yet progressed to Stage 3. Relate your comments to the indicators, using the model Priority Statement that follows.

Step 3

SETTING PRIORITIES

Consult Chapter III for a description of the priorities appropriate to your parish's stage of development. Taking these priorities as a benchmark, develop your own set of priorities as circumstances dictate. For example, the first priority in Stage 2 is Catholic nurture, and the second is organizing ministries of outreach to the community at large. If your parish is already strong on nurture but has little outreach, you may wish to make outreach your own first priority.

Using this process and following the model provided, draw up a list of priorities arranged in order of importance. The resulting Priority Statement should be rather general, and need not include detailed material on practical implentation. It will prove to be an excellent starting point for planning the specific activities and programs that are to be emphasized in a given year.

II

Sample Priority Statement for
St. Joseph's Church, Magnolia, Alabama
June 1, 19___

I

PROGRESS REPORT

St. Joseph's Parish in the Diocese of Exopolis comprises the entire counties of Smith and Jones in Alabama. There is a mission congregation at Peachtree in Jones County, but this report considers only the congregation at Magnolia, along with Smith County.

Smith County, covering 1,579 square miles, has 18,620 people, of whom 220 (1.1 percent) are Catholics at least occasional in religious practice, 14,320 (76.9 percent) are Protestants, and 4,080 (22.0 percent) are unchurched. Between 19___ and 19___ the county population grew 3.6 percent, mostly because of new jobs related to manufacturing. Industry is the basis of the local economy. Manufacturing establishments, including representatives of the meat packing, boiler making, textile, sporting goods and furniture industries, employ 37.2 percent of the work force. In addition, the area has many small farms, which produce cotton, soybeans, timber, hay, dairy and beef cattle, and hogs. Only 7.3 percent of the work force, however, is engaged in full-time farming. Poverty is extremely high; 25.9 percent of the families have incomes below the official government poverty line for the county. Blacks represent half the population (49.4 percent); one-half of the Black families (51.2 percent) are in poverty.

PARISH PROGRAMS

1. NURTURE OF CATHOLICS

Worship. The Sunday liturgy is celebrated at Magnolia on Saturday evening and twice on Sunday morning. Confessions are heard before all Masses or by appointment. A special Penance service is held twice a year. The daily Mass and homily is attended by 15-20 persons consistently. Devotions are held during May and

October. As part of these devotions, members of the CYO come as a group to visit the Blessed Sacrament one night a week. On first Fridays, parishioners participate in 24 hours of adoration, either at home or in church. During part of that time the Blessed Sacrament is exposed in church, and Benediction is held. Parishioners frequently make visits to the Blessed Sacrament. There is a prayer group of eight people who have made the Cursillo. The Liturgical Committee participates in planning the celebration of major feasts, and promotes home prayer by distributing meal prayers and leaflets containing passages of Scripture. These programs are under the direct administration of the pastor, assisted by members of the Liturgical Committee and a Sister who is on the parish staff. As parishioners gain more experience, they will assume more responsibility in planning Sunday liturgies. However, it is visualized that the Sister will remain on the staff even after the parish has completed the missionary stage, in order to assist the Committee in liturgical music and other areas in which she has particular expertise. Funding for this will come from normal parish revenue.

Christian Education for Children. Grade school children have an hour's class Tuesdays after school, taught by four parishioners and the staff Sister. High school students have a 50-minute weekly class between the two Sunday Masses. The Sister teaches grades 8 and 9 and the pastor grades 10-12. There is a summer Bible School for grades 1-7, which lasts two weeks and includes 30 hours of instruction. The Sister serves as coordinator for these programs and trains the other teachers. Course content is under the direct supervision of the pastor. The Sister will remain on the staff even after the parish has completed the missionary stage; funding will come from normal parish revenue.

Adult Education. The pastor conducts adult education classes in the spring (6-8 weeks) on Monday evenings. Various topics are selected: Scripture, evangelization, spiritual life, social justice, family problems and the like. Usually 30-40 adults attend. On the second Wednesday of each month there is a discussion group from 9:30 to 11:00 a.m. on current events and their moral implications. These sessions are led by the pastor, and 15-16 persons regularly participate. In addition, the pastor gives instruction at the monthly Cursillo meeting.

Life Events. The Sacraments relating to life events (Baptism, Confirmation, Anointing of the Sick, Matrimony) are regularly celebrated. There is a program of regular pastoral visitation, including the sick. Counseling and spiritual direction, when requested, are provided at the parish center. Both the pastor and the staff Sister participate in counseling. One of the objectives for the future is to encourage parishioners to support one another through spiritual encouragement in times of crisis.

Intensification. There is a parish day of recollection once a month. A parish mission is held every three years, with the help of an outside preacher. The parish regularly encourages parishioners to participate in the Cursillo, and twenty persons have participated so far. These twenty meet monthly for prayer and support. A lay person serves as chairman.

Youth Ministry. The CYO is very active; its membership includes 19 out of a possible 27 teenagers. The CYO meets weekly and carries out an extensive program of service, prayer and recreation. One of the teenagers serves as president, and a young adult serves as adviser and moderator.

Women. The parish branch of the Catholic Women's Society actively promotes many parish projects and programs. Among its many activities, it provides a welcome to newly-arrived Catholics through its Welcoming Committee. A laywoman serves as president of the CWS, and the advisor is the staff Sister.

Socials. The parish holds occasional social events in order to cement relationships among Catholics and strengthen their faith through mutual association. These events are sponsored alternately by the Catholic Women's Society, the CYO and the parish council.

2. SEEKING CHRISTIAN UNITY.

Ministries of Friendliness. There is a general feeling of good will among the churches, and this is enhanced through the ministerial association, in which the pastor participates and which he has served as president.

Congregational Contact. At least once a year there is an exchange of visits with the United Methodists for discussion and a devotional. Twice a year the pastor gives an information course on Catholic doctrine in Black churches. He also gives similar courses to individual Black families on request.

Prayer for Unity. The parish participates in the annual community Thanksgiving service and in noon services during Holy Week. These events are sponsored by the ministerial association.

3. EVANGELIZING THE UNCHURCHED

Prayer. Once a year, during the May devotions, there is a formal prayer service for the unchurched. Evangelization is frequently mentioned in the Prayer of the Faithful.

Supporting Ministries. Parishioners are urged to invite their friends to church, and from time to time some of them do.

Organized Ministries. The staff Sister regularly visits homes in the area to deliver brochures about the Church. The plan is to encourage parishioners to participate in this ministry, and Sister is currently making efforts in this direction. After the parish is no longer in the missionary stage, this type of activity will be entirely in the hands of the laity.

Educational Experiences. Special courses are offered to Black unchurched persons, and a Bible School is regularly held each summer for their children. The pastor conducts the courses, and the staff Sister conducts the summer Bible School, with the help of two parishioners and four outside lay volunteers. The plan is to increase local lay participation in the Bible Schools, if possible by involving the CYO. After the parish has passed from the missionary stage, the Sister will be available only for coordination of the school's program.

Media Ministry. Every week there is a five-minute taped meditation on the radio that is directed toward the unchurched. Advertisements are placed in the newspapers and an article is written about every seven weeks. The pastor conducts these activities.

4. SOCIAL ACTION

MINISTRY TO IMMEDIATE NEEDS

Prayer. During Advent, the parish prays especially for those whose human dignity is lessened because they are suffering material or emotional needs.

Supporting Ministries. Parishioners are urged, especially during Advent, to see Christ in their neighbors in the community and respond to their needs.

Sponsorship. The parish was involved in establishing and funding a day care center, which is now community operated. From time to time, it participates in such projects.

Organized Parish Ministries. The Catholic Women's Society tithes its income, and the parish as a whole tithes its income for St. Vincent's Charitable Fund. The money is used for community needs: helping a family whose home has burned, helping a young person who could not otherwise go to college, assisting with medical expenses, contributing to the community park or library. St. Vincent's Fund is administered by a lay committee elected by the parish membership at large. The pastor serves as adviser and source of accountability. In addition, the Catholic Women's Society visits the nursing homes and prepares Christmas baskets. The CYO does Christmas caroling in hospitals and nursing homes and sponsors poor families. The parish council has sponsored several families from Vietnam.

MINISTRY TO SOCIAL SYSTEMS

Prayer. Prayer for justice is included in the Advent prayer theme.

Education. At least once a year, the theme of a newspaper article is Catholic teaching on social issues. The pastor occasionally addresses the Lion's Club on a similar theme.

Supporting Ministries. Education for responsible social action is a constant theme in homilies and adult courses, as well as in the Christian education program in general. For example, a number of sermons have been given about racial justice. At least a few Catholics participate as individuals in social programs sponsored by citizens' groups, with a consciousness that in so doing they are engaging in the lay apostolate.

5. CATHOLICITY (CONCERN FOR THE WIDER CHURCH).

Prayer. During October the parish prayer theme is missions and vocations.

Education. During October, sermons and instructions are given about the work of the diocese and world missions, and the need for vocations.

Supporting Ministries. Parishioners are encouraged to serve on diocesan committees, and four of them do so.

Financial. For the past five years the parish has contributed between 14 and 20 percent of its total regular expenditures to diocesan collections.

THE PARISH AS A COMMUNITY

1. HISTORY. The congregation at Magnolia was established in 19__. The church was built in 19__ and the parish hall in 19__.

2. SIZE. There are 220 parishioners, of whom 207 are regular in religious practice and 13 are occasional. Catholics represent 1.1 percent of the total population of Smith County.

3. SPIRITUALITY. At least half the parishioners have a strong Catholic identity, have internalized their religion, and have a vision of ministry that includes outreach beyond the Catholic community. Through the years, prayer has come to permeate the parish's life. This is attributed to the gradually increasing activities centered on the Mass and devotion to Christ in the Blessed Sacrament.

4. LOCAL ROOTS. During the past five years the parish gained 69 persons. There was one death, two persons moved away, and one person left the Catholic Church. However, 11 babies were baptized, there were 11 converts, 15 returned to religious practice, and 36

Catholics moved into the area. Considering the development of industry in the area, the Catholic population will probably remain rather stable, with perhaps a slight increase year by year.

The social characteristics of Catholics, however, are not typical of the county as a whole. There are only four Black Catholics, in a county where 49.4 percent of the population is Black. More than half the Catholics (54.7 percent) are newcomers to the area since 1965, compared to 12.4 percent in the county as a whole. Catholics are overrepresented in the higher income brackets and underrepresented in the lower brackets. The percent of white collar workers among Catholics is greater (65.1) than in the county as a whole (23.1).

5. STAFF. The parish is served by the pastor and one Sister. For the past six years, two or three summer volunteers have assisted in various programs. The same staff is anticipated when the parish has passed beyond the missionary stage, with the possible exception of the summer volunteers.

6. PARTICIPATION. About half the Catholics participate in formal parish programs of nurture and outreach as active ministers. There is a leadership group of about 12 adults. Informal spiritual ministry from one lay person to another, however, is notably lacking. At least 20 percent participate informally as individual Christians in ministries of outreach, especially in social action. Lay participation in ecumenism and evangelization is minimal.

7. COMMUNITY OPENNESS. The parish presently has no plans for structuring the Catholic community to embrace persons of diverse ethnic/racial groups and all social classes, including the poor. This question has not yet come up for consideration.

8. FINANCES. The parish has received help in the past, both for programs and for buildings. For the past five years, however, it has been able to fund its own local ministries, and pay the salaries of the pastor and the staff Sister. Funding is not unduly dependent on a few, and is considered to be stable. There is little likelihood of increasing local funding until the number of parishioners increases.

9. FACILITIES. The parish has a church capable of seating 130, a

parish hall, a rectory, and adequate grounds for parking. There is a debt of $13,000, but interest and principal payments are being met through current local revenues.

10. PLANNING. The parish council is active and well organized. There is no overall planning at present, but council members do plan for all the individual programs. A system of reporting has been set up for each program whereby the pastor and council can exercise supervision. Since the parish is so small, communication is mostly informal. Except for the parish bulletin, there is no formal communications system.

2

PRESENT STAGE OF DEVELOPMENT

Our parish is in the third stage of development. The basic Sacramental and educational ministries are well organized, and the parishioners have at least occasional opportunities to participate in programs of spiritual intensification such as missions, days of recollection and Cursillos. The level of spirituality and breadth of vision in the parish is good; consequently, we do have a vital and effective parish council. Ministries of ecumenism, evangelization of the unchurched, social action, and concern for the wider Church are ongoing and organized. Quite a few parishioners are actively involved in parish ministries of nurture and outreach, and some are exercising leadership in such ministries as the Catholic Women's Society and the CYO.

On the other hand, we have not yet achieved the level of development required for the completion of Stage 3. Although the Catholic community is stable and self-sustaining, there are not enough of us to provide a good diversification in ministry. We notice this especially in the Christian Education Program, where the children are too few to warrant separate classes for each grade level. The Catholic Church does not yet have deep enough roots in the county. For example, although half the population of the county is Black, there are only four Black members of the Catholic Church. In a county characterized by a blue collar population, the Catholic parish is composed primarily of white collar workers. We have many organized ministries of nurture and outreach, but some of them are so underdeveloped that, taken together, they do not constitute a "full range." For example, there is no contact whatsoever with the largest denomination in the county, the

Southern Baptists. We certainly do qualify as having spiritual vitality, both in the lives of many of our members and in our group life; St. Joseph's is a parish that prays. Yet the involvement of the laity in parish ministries, although excellent, needs enlarging in several areas. This applies especially to ministries of ecumenism and evangelization of the unchurched.

3

PRIORITIES

Considering our present stage of development, our first priority is to become more deeply rooted in the community. We are already reaching out to evangelize the unchurched, especially the poor. But we need to devise some practical plan for welcoming them as Catholics as soon as Our Lord touches their hearts with the grace of unity with the Church. We do not know just how to do this, or what structures might be appropriate. But our first effort will be to discuss the problem prayerfully, in our parish council and with the congregation as a whole.

Our second priority is to increase the active involvement of parishioners in outreach. In ecumenism, we need to make at least initial contact with the Southern Baptist Churches. In evangelization, we need to find a more effective way of reaching the unchurched. In social action, we need to help members of the parish reflect on what they might do in their everyday lives to improve the social climate, especially in the area of racial justice.

Our third priority is to move into general planning in the parish council. In doing this, we will be building on the good experience we have had in coordinating the parish's individual apostolic programs. As we now turn our attention to the larger issues, we hope to become more responsive to God's Will and the mission of the Church.

Appendix B

Correlative Ministries

The Church cannot be fully present in a locality unless the people who live there have practical access to a Eucharistic community in which, through ministries of Word and Sacrament, they can satisfy all their ordinary, everyday spiritual needs and reach out in ministry to the community at large. The parish remains always the centerpiece of the Church's missionary activity.

There is more to missionary activity, however, than forming local Eucharistic communities, however essential that might be. Part of the task of localizing the Church is accomplished through "correlative ministries" which, although not a substitute for the parish, have their own important contribution to make. Through them, the Church is present in an area in ways that are distinct from, but complementary to, the work of the parish. Such ministries have traditionally played a significant role in the overall missionary activity of the Church.

Correlative ministries may be thought of as falling into three groups:

TYPE 1. LOCAL MINISTRIES. Local non-parochial ministries exist side-by-side with the parish in a relatively small geographic area. Examples would be houses of prayer, small clinics, housing ministries, organizations providing social services to the poor, ministries of presence and the like. These ministries often respond to particular and urgent needs of a special group, with a concentration beyond the capacity of a parish community that must necessarily be concerned with general needs. Although it is not their primary purpose, such correlative ministries often provide an apostolic outlet for parishioners who cooperate in their work. The resulting heightened sense of Christian responsibility is bound to deepen and intensify parish life. In addition, the witness they give often encourages a more favorable attitude toward the Church and contributes to evangelization.

TYPE 2. SUPPORTING MINISTRIES. These support the ministry of parishes (and sometimes other apostolates in the Church). For the parish they can provide teacher training, lay leadership development, adult education, retreats, youth programs, parish missions, training in lay evangelization and the like. Often these ministries are organized at a diocesan or deanery level, although they may be found at the national or regional level as well. Without the assistance of these supporting ministries, a parish can only with difficulty carry out its proper work.

TYPE 3. LARGE-SCALE MINISTRIES. These are set up in a relatively large geographic area to meet particular apostolic needs. Their ministry is immediate and direct. Examples would be media evangelization efforts, large-scale justice ministries, social service agencies, hospitals, colleges, national or regional ecumenical dialogues and the like. Large-scale ministries are sometimes combined with Type 2 ministries in a given church structure or agency. Although distinct from the local Eucharistic community, they have an important, if indirect, effect on its work. They help create a climate of acceptance for Catholicism, they address important needs, and they provide opportunities for parishioners to participate in the work of the wider Church.